🍂 TO SET BEFORE THE KING 🍂

THE IOWA
SZATHMÁRY
CULINARY ARTS SERIES

Edited by David E. Schoonover

Katharina Schratt's Festive Recipes

TO

Edited by Gertrud Graubart Champe

SET

Translated by Paula von Haimberger Arno

BEFORE

In collaboration with Chef Louis Szathmáry

THE

Foreword by David E. Schoonover

KING

University of Iowa Press Ψ *Iowa City*

University of Iowa Press,

Iowa City 52242

Copyright © 1996 by the

University of Iowa Press

All rights reserved

Printed in the United States of America

Design by Richard Hendel

The recipes in this book have not been tested

by the publisher.

Printed on acid-free paper

Library of Congress Cataloging-in-Publication Data

To set before the king: Katharina Schratt's festive recipes / edited by

Gertrud Graubart Champe; translated by Paula von Haimberger Arno in

collaboration with Louis Szathmáry; foreword by David E. Schoonover.

p. cm.—(The Iowa Szathmáry culinary arts series)

Translated from the German.

Includes bibliographical references and index.

ISBN 0-87745-535-X (cloth)

1. Cookery, Austrian.   2. Cookery, Hungarian.   3. Schratt,

Katharina, 1855–1940.   I. Champe, Gertrud Graubart.   II. Arno,

Paula von Haimberger.   III. Szathmáry, Louis.   IV. Series.

TX721.T62   1996

641.59436—dc20   95-45507

                                                            CIP

01   00   99   98   97   96   C   5   4   3   2   1

CONTENTS

Foreword
David E. Schoonover
vii

Introduction: Katharina Schratt
Gertrud Graubart Champe
1

Cookbook, 1905
Translated by Paula von Haimberger Arno
49

Notes
Gertrud Graubart Champe
107

Bring Vienna to Your Table!
Chef Louis Szathmáry
119

Index
219

FOREWORD

David E. Schoonover

Many readers and collectors of cookbooks now agree with the *New York Times* that "Prose, Not Recipes, Sells Today's Food Books" (May 15, 1991) and that "The History of Food [Has Gained] a Scholarly Pedigree" (May 30, 1984).

The cookbooks appearing in our series are selected from the University of Iowa Libraries' Szathmáry Collection of Culinary Arts, which contains more than 20,000 items: printed books dating from 1499 to 1995, more than a hundred culinary manuscripts, some 3,500 ephemeral pamphlets and booklets, and a selection of professional and popular magazines.

The Szathmáry Collection is an extraordinarily varied trove, presenting more than five hundred years' worth of books and manuscripts on all aspects of food and its history. Our series provides today's readers and collectors with much more than recipes. Many of these cookbooks contain introductions, perhaps literary or historical matter, period advertisements, or a variety of illustrations that are interesting in themselves. The cultural context of cookbooks is also important — who prepared or published them, for what audience, in what time period?

To Set before the King is the first translation from a manuscript to appear in our series, and, given the nature of this particular manuscript, the contributors to this volume have provided appropriate historical, social, political, economic, artistic, and culinary background. "The king" is Franz Joseph I, emperor of Austria and king of Hungary. The manuscript belonged to the actress Katharina Schratt, whom the emperor addressed as "My dear, good Friend." It is not in her handwriting. Our contributors speculate on who may have written it and for what purposes it may have been prepared. It was undoubtedly intended for private use but is now made available to a much wider readership.

Gertrud Graubart Champe and Paula von Haimberger Arno are native-born Austrians; Chef Louis Szathmáry is a native of Hungary. They are intimately familiar with the countries, languages, cuisines, and customs of the Austro-Hungarian Empire. Gertrud Champe's introduction provides not only a full discussion of the Schratt manuscript but also brings to life the very real personalities connected with it. Paula Arno's translation gives an accurate and delicious rendering of the text. Louis Szathmáry's vivid invitation to "Bring Vienna to Your Table!" captures the multiplicity of flavors from the world that he knows and loves.

Royalties from sales of volumes in the series assist the University of Iowa Libraries in purchasing books to enhance the Szathmáry Collection of Culinary Arts. Forthcoming volumes will include an American culinary yearbook containing literary quotations and recipes for every day of the year and an early nineteenth-century English compendium of "Universal Knowledge and Experience."

TO SET BEFORE THE KING

🧩 INTRODUCTION: 🧩
KATHARINA SCHRATT

Gertrud Graubart Champe

Sometime after 1970, at an estate auction in London, there sur-
faced a manuscript written in German, containing more than two
hundred recipes for elegant snacks, main dishes, and a wealth of
desserts, ices, and punches. These recipes are recorded in a
stitched, ruled student's notebook covered with the traditional
black-and-white marbled paper and labeled "*Kochbuch*, 1905."
Inside the notebook is the penciled notation "aus dem Besitz
Kath. Schratt's" (Property of Kath. Schratt). On the first page,
faint traces of a pressed four-leaf clover can still be seen, and lying
between the pages, on a loose sheet, are three recipes in a different hand, each for a kind of tea cake called a gugelhupf.

This notebook, a concrete bit of information from the para-
doxical world of turn-of-the-century Vienna, belonged to a
woman who played an extraordinary role in her society. Born in
comfortable circumstances at a comfortable time in Vienna, she
was propelled out of her agreeable surroundings and into the
public world by her passion and talent for the theater. She became the toast of every city she played in and numbered among
her ardent admirers crowned heads, great industrialists, artists,
and composers. She caught the eye of the emperor of Austria and
king of Hungary, Franz Joseph I, and in a relationship that was in
fact arranged by his wife, Empress Elisabeth, Katharina Schratt
became the emperor's friend, companion, and confidante for the
thirty-two years between their meeting and the day he died.

Katharina Schratt was born on September 11, 1853, in Baden
bei Wien, a health spa just outside Vienna. Lying on the river
Schwechat, the town goes back to the days of the Roman colo-
nization, when the area's warm water, bubbling out of dolomite
limestone, was already appreciated for medicinal baths. By the

1

time Katharina was born, the town's population was sixteen thousand, and thousands of people were coming to Baden each year to take the sulfur-rich waters, stroll through the woods, and listen to bands playing in the park.

The Schratt family was of the busy, productive middle class. Anton, Katharina's father, was a successful dry goods merchant and kept a livery stable. As was quite natural for a respected businessman, he held various public offices. Katharina Wallner, his wife, was the daughter of the fire chief of Baden, who was a descendant of a prosperous Hungarian landowning family. John Chrysostom Schratt, Katharina's paternal grandfather, had come to Vienna as a young man from his home in Constance to study surgery and obstetrics. He married the daughter of an antiquarian book dealer who was supplier to the Imperial Court and settled down to practice in Baden. He did much of his work *pro bono publico*, for which he received an imperial decoration. His interest in the welfare of his fellow citizens included not only a medical practice but forward-looking efforts toward public sanitation. It was due to his work that open sewers were abolished in Baden and that the city walls were torn down to expedite the removal of refuse. In these and other ways, members of the Schratt family became part of the fabric of their society, and in time Katharina found her remarkable way to contribute to the culture as well.

Katharina's childhood was sheltered and firmly religious. She was fascinated by the theater at an early age, and in a little memoir she wrote for a popular newspaper in 1887, she confessed that at the age of six she was already passionately set on being an actress. As she tells the story, she plotted with a schoolmate, an actor's child, and won the opportunity to make an impromptu appearance in a spectacle called *Deborah* at the arena in her hometown. Her first official performance, with a mention in the program and a review in the newspaper, came in an amateur theatrical when she was fifteen. The reviewers declared that Kathi was adorable and that she knew how to place her personality at the service of the play. This set the tone for the glowing reviews she would receive during a stage career of almost forty years.

Although Anton Schratt had been stagestruck as a young man, he joined in his wife's vigorous opposition to Katharina's ambition for the stage. This is not surprising; the stage was not an admired career. For most women, it meant a loose and precarious life, an endless round of dreary provincial tours and one-night stands. Until or unless an actress or dancer was married, her only hope for a secure life was to become the mistress of a generous man. Because of these concerns, Kathi was eventually sent off to school to keep her mind off the stage, but to no avail. The girl was miserable away from home and begged to be allowed to come back. When she was sixteen, her parents bowed to her unrelenting campaign and allowed her to enroll in the Kirschner Academy in Vienna, a theater school directed by a former actor at the Imperial and Royal Court Theater. When she acted in performances open to the public, the young student was showered with praise for her comedic charm in reviews that predicted a brilliant future for her.

After her graduation from drama school, there was lively bidding for Katharina's services in Vienna, and she flew from one audition to another, chaperoned by her relatives. But she got a better offer from the Imperial Court Theater in Berlin, where the director decided that, if everyone was running after her, he would not be making much of a mistake in hiring her without the usual probationary period. In Berlin, the young actress was a great success; her Austrian speech and style gave her charm a slightly exotic touch. She captured the hearts of all her audiences and was well loved by the general theater-going public as well as by Emperor Wilhelm I, who is said to have enjoyed all her performances tremendously.

But the admiration of Germany did not capture Schratt's loyalty. When the director of the Stadttheater in Vienna made her a new and more generous offer, reflecting her success in Berlin, she did not hesitate to pull up stakes and return to Vienna. Of course her behavior unleashed bitter and costly breach of contract proceedings, but being back in Vienna seemed well worth the price.

Katharina began her work with the Stadttheater on March 4, 1873. In the twelve months that followed, she performed thirty different roles, including Kate in *Taming of the Shrew*, Margarethe in *Faust*, and leads in a broad repertoire of German, Austrian, and French comedies. Under the tutelage of Heinrich Laube, the director of the theater, Katharina's acting increased in scope and polish, and she was well on her way to becoming an accomplished ingenue. Both for her charm and her talent, she was soon the darling of the town. On tour, she took the Imperial Court of Russia by storm and was feted in all the cities of the Austro-Hungarian Empire to which her travels brought her. A newspaper critic called her "God's masterpiece," and the Viennese author Stephan Zweig declared that she belonged to the whole city.

And oh, what a city it was! Vienna in the second half of the nineteenth century was a glittering world of activity, drawing money and people from all over Europe into the whirlwind of creative industry later known as the "Age of the Founders." The forces that were causing the unexpectedly great and rapid growth of Vienna had been building for some time. As perhaps the most glamorous capital of the German Federation, Vienna had been drawing visitors from all over Europe, who came to study, to work, to buy, or to play. The mechanical and industrial revolution was fueling the inventiveness of little manufacturing industries on the outskirts of the city. Ambitious young people from outlying regions of the empire were coming to the capital, some in coaches, some on the railroad, to seek success. The spirit of the times was on the move toward urbanization.

But the city of Vienna was on the brink of choking on its own growth, enclosed as it was by its city wall. This fortification, a creation of the Middle Ages, had last been of significant use in the late seventeenth century in battles against the Turks. By the middle of the nineteenth century, its destruction had been considered by at least three monarchs. The summit of the wall, wide enough to turn a coach and four, had been given over to foot and carriage traffic, the moat around it was picturesquely overgrown, and the glacis on the far side of the moat had been largely turned into park land where the whole city could take the air. At Christmastime in 1857, Franz Joseph, in a proclamation beginning "It is my will," ordered the old wall to be torn down and a major effort to be mounted for the expansion and beautification of the Imperial Residence City. The start of this work of urbanization marked the end of *Alt Wien*, Old Vienna, a time and place which seem dreamlike today, where deep countryside began immediately at the edge of the city and the middle class obediently knew its place.

A worldwide design competition was announced to elicit a plan according to which Vienna might be modernized. The emperor chose a concept calling for a belt road, the *Ringstraße*, around the ancient inner city. Carl Schorske, in his collection of essays *Fin-de-Siècle Vienna*, has explained in satisfying detail how the architecture of Vienna's Ring became an expression of the political ideals of the day, starting from the emperor's point of view and then going on from there in ebullient progress. For our story, it might be enough to say that the prodigious construction of new buildings around the Ring was driven by more than the entrepreneurial instinct. Investing money in a considerable and luxurious private residence, or "apartment palace," on the Ring earned its builder the favor of the emperor, for whom this new creation had become a favorite project. Living along this bright new street, its facades glittering with windows and displaying a rich mixture of historical styles, meant seeing and being seen, for this was the place where almost everybody who was anybody wanted to live. It was the one place where the withdrawn and distant feudal aristocrats, some tracing their ancestry to the thirteenth century and beyond, were willing to be seen side by side with the families who had been swept into prosperity by the new growth. Otherwise, the separation was meticulously preserved. It is true that much power was beginning to slide toward where the money was, but social distinctions were relentlessly maintained. The families of ancient title closed ranks against the rich and clever people who had breathed new energy into the city and were gradually changing the face of Vienna. Many of these bringers of modern times — industrialists, inventors, scholars, lawyers, specialists in various branches of government — had been granted titles of nobility by the emperor and constituted what has been called the service nobility. Although the grander, older families were willing to have business dealings with the newer ones, no social exchange was desired. Rather, the old families maintained the same high decorum, away from the hubbub and prying eyes, as the Imperial Court, where they were received by right of birth. This was the First Society, people who represented the highest standard but were no longer, as they once had been, at the forefront. The Second Society, on the other hand — the rich, the powerful, the talented, the famous, and occasionally the notorious — was avidly taking advantage of the ferment, amenities, and bright horizons on offer.

While Vienna was growing into a brilliant, modern world capital, in Europe the Hapsburg monarchy had been losing ground for most of the nineteenth century. In 1806, at the insistence of Napoleon I, Emperor Francis I of Austria resigned the title of Holy Roman Emperor, and the empire was dissolved. It was replaced with a confederation of thirty-nine German-speaking states, called first the Confederation of the Rhine and then the German Confederation. In 1866, after a series of catastrophic military losses, culminating in the battle of Königgrätz in 1866, this confederation was dissolved again and re-formed, but without Austria. In this way, Franz Joseph lost, once and for all, Austria's position of power and influence in the German-speaking world. Germany went its way toward unification, with Berlin as its center of gravity, and Austria was left to its own devices. In 1867 Hapsburg lands suffered a great and unprecedented division when Hungary, a vast area including at the time Transylvania, Slovakia, Ruthenia, Croatia, Slovenia, and the Banat, was declared to have a separate existence from the empire, equal in status with Austria and separate from it. The resulting political entity was Austria-Hungary, and Franz Joseph became both emperor of Austria and apostolic king of Hungary. Smaller and weaker, Austria turned its face more and more to the south and east, becoming the Danube monarchy. Vienna, instead of being a capital of a great confederation, was now a royal capital and residence city only, center of a country attempting to exist as a multinational state. As the social chronicler Frederic Morton puts it, the whole gamut of voices sounded there, from yodelers to muezzins. Playing out its new orientation, the city turned inward and concentrated on itself, growing in brilliance, like a star in the process of burning itself out.

This is the world where Katharina Schratt was at home, admired, sought after, and talked about. At the Stadttheater, her name on the playbill ensured a full house, and night after night she played all the great roles she had learned in school and in Berlin. A short while after her return to Vienna, the stock market crash of 1873 compromised the funding of the Stadttheater, which was private and not subsidized by the Crown. When the theater closed because of financial losses suffered by its backers, Kathi accepted a call to the German Court Theater of the czar of Russia, where she was a great success and the delight of all. But this woman, who was an embodiment of Viennese charm and humor and popular culture, could not stay away from the wellspring too long, and so, as soon as the finances of the Stadttheater were again in good repair, Kathi came back. At the stage door, lines of admirers formed to ask for autographs. On tour, students unhitched her horses and drew her carriage through the streets in triumph. At home in Vienna, she was living in an elegant apartment on the *Ringstraße*, entertaining, buying clothes and jewelry hand over fist, and preferring fun to prudence.

On September 25, 1879, after months of rumors and wondering, Katharina Schratt married Nikolaus Kiss de Itebbe, member of a noble Hungarian family with immense landholdings and a significant military and political history. Kiss was a much-traveled diplomat who, in the words of the actress's niece, Katharina Hryntschak, cut a dashing figure with his monocle and his perpetually tanned skin, like a pasha in a picture book. It can be imagined what a stir it caused when the woman desired by half of

Vienna married, and not even in a large, public ceremony. This match was not a fairy-tale marriage, however. No one believed that she had married for love; it had clearly been for money. Presumably she was not only trying, as usual, to settle her own debts — the endless bills for clothing, jewelry, and entertainment had become quite unmanageable — but was also hoping to help her father, who had fallen on difficult times. Marrying a member of a family with considerable agricultural land would be an excellent way to achieve this goal, but unfortunately, her husband was not what he seemed. His own creditors were so eager to seize him that they followed the happy pair on their honeymoon.

Shortly after her marriage, Katharina declared that her career was at an end, that she would leave the stage and devote her life to her husband. A son, Anton, was born a year later. However, a chronological record of her theater credits shows that Schratt soon resumed her successful career and a life very much on her own. By this time, it was clear that since both husband and wife were notorious spendthrifts, they could never survive by relying on each other. They remained married until Nikolaus died in 1909, but during all those years, the actress and the consul led distinctly separate lives. This circumstance had much less gossip value than one might expect since, in any case, Baron Kiss was kept out of the country by his diplomatic duties for long periods of time.

In 1882 Schratt was invited as a guest artist to the Thalia, an outstanding German-language theater in New York. In her usual style, she won over the audience during her month-long engagement and was offered many inducements to stay. But Vienna, as always, was where she wanted to be. Within a few months of her return, after some strenuous haggling, Katharina was offered a two-year contract at the Imperial and Royal Court Theater (*Burgtheater*), which represented the pinnacle of every Austrian actor's ambition. However, the offer in itself was not enough to make the young woman's dream come true. Not surprisingly, her apparent inability to stay out of debt was a near-fatal obstacle. In spite of the fact that by this time she was already very well paid,

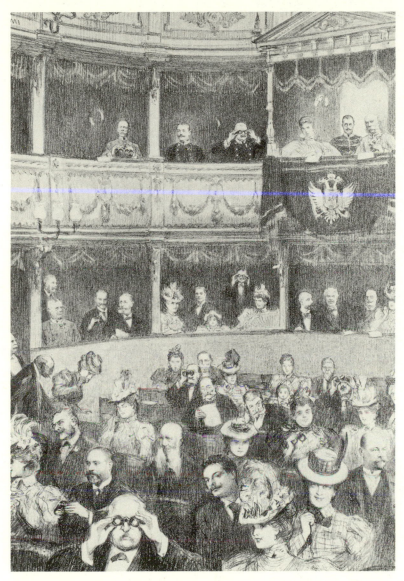

An evening at the *Burgtheater*. Many of the faces in the audience are portraits of society figures of the day. The emperor sat in the imperial loge only on formal occasions. When he came for his own pleasure—for instance, to see a new performance by Katharina Schratt—he sat in the so-called incognito loge, much nearer the stage. From *Viribus Unitis* (Vienna, 1911).

Katharina could never quite keep up with her dressmaker bills, the costs of her elegant apartment, and the drain on her purse of entertaining in a style that suited her reputation and popularity. In order to be engaged at the Court Theater, an actor had to be of demonstrably good character and free of debts. At the moment when the Court Theater appointment hung in the balance, the amount of her indebtedness was the equivalent of $100,000. A photograph of Kathi, dated 1878, bears eloquent witness to her plight, as well as to her sweet optimism that someone would always bail her out. The twenty-five-year-old beauty looks out of the frame with a curly lipped half-smile and deeply shaded eyes, bare arms white and rounded, and hair decorated with a delectable concoction of flowers and butterflies. All around the mat of the photograph she has written, "Fingers crossed!!! Fingers crossed!!! Fingers crossed!!! Who will pay my debts?" In 1882 it was Eduard Palmer, the industrialist, she turned to, a rich bachelor about town who surrounded himself with actresses and women who called themselves actresses. He was very glad to help out, but not wanting to spend all his money on one actress, he took up a collection among his friends and even managed to get the last $35,000 from the director of the emperor's privy purse, on the grounds that it was a necessary investment in good theater.

By November 1883 Schratt was a member of the Court Theater, playing some great and some small comic roles. She was successful, sought after, and had a secure place in the popular culture and social life of Vienna. And yet we would never remember her today were it not for her association with the emperor Franz Joseph, which began around this time and lasted for the next thirty-two years until the day he died. Indeed, every serious study of the second half of the emperor's reign mentions Katharina Schratt as his mainstay through tragedy, political disasters, and the frailty of old age.

Franz Joseph saw Katharina Schratt for the first time in 1873, when she played Kate in *The Taming of the Shrew* at a performance to celebrate the silver jubilee of his reign. There is no

Emperor Franz Joseph I as an elegant man of fifty-four, two years be-
fore he was presented with Katharina Schratt's portrait. From Eugene
Bagger, *Franz Joseph: Eine Persönlichkeit-Studie* (Zürich, Leipzig, Wien:
Amalthea-Verlag).

record that she made any particular impression on him. The actress and the Emperor met for the first time in 1883, on the occasion of her engagement at the Court Theater. An audience for a newly appointed actor was the normal protocol at the court of Franz Joseph. Indeed, the conscientious ruler held endless rounds of these audiences, in which he greeted people who were contributing in some way to the cultural, educational, or economic life of the empire. For the thirty-year-old actress, however, this audience at Schönbrunn Palace, the emperor's summer residence, was anything but ordinary, and she prepared for it with great care by consulting a friend accustomed to court ceremonial. In the course of practicing for the event with her adviser, Katharina plunked herself down in a chair, for which she was roundly scolded, on the grounds that she must remain standing in the emperor's presence. On the day of the audience, she arrived at the palace well dressed and well rehearsed.

She began her speech: "Your Majesty has been pleased to . . ."

The emperor interrupted with, "Won't you take a seat, Fräulein Schratt?"

Once again the actress tried to recite her rehearsed speech: "Your Majesty has been pleased to . . ."

And again the Emperor interrupted, asking, "Fräulein Schratt, just why won't you take a seat?"

"Schulz told me I'd better not dare!" blurted the discountenanced young woman.

The conversation was a little more relaxed and lively after that; in fact, functionaries outside the audience chamber were astounded to hear the emperor, a very solemn man, laughing heartily and often. Many years later, in 1896, when they were already fast friends and exchanging stories about their daily lives, the emperor wrote to Katharina Schratt about the 128 audiences he had granted the day before and teased her gently about the fact that none of the ladies he had welcomed had been as shy as "someone else" had been at her first audience.

A few weeks after this first audience, Katharina had occasion to request another. This time, she addressed the emperor on behalf of her estranged husband, in a matter having to do with his family's estates and wealth in Transylvania. In 1848, at the time of the revolution, which was the first great event of his reign, Franz Joseph had ordered the execution of the Hungarian leaders at the insistence of his mother, the regent. In 1867, however, when Austria concluded the compromise with Hungary known as the *Ausgleich*, Franz Joseph attempted to make amends for the ruthless reprisals of 1848–1849. He regretted the executions bitterly and was known to have said to his wife that, if he could, he would reclaim the dead officers from the grave with his own ten fingers. As part of the reparations, confiscated estates were returned to the survivors of the executed leaders. Among these was the von Kiss family; Ernö von Kiss, the uncle of Nikolaus, had been a general and for a time the commander of all the Hungarian revolutionary forces. The estates had indeed been returned, but the von Kiss family had squandered them and was once again penniless. Katharina's request was that the family be granted a sum to equal what the family would in fact have earned from its holdings between 1848 and 1867. Franz Joseph, who had a very low tolerance for poor management, did not grant Katharina's request. After all, he did not yet have any connection to her.

The two did not see each other again until two years later, when they met at a ball during the carnival season. Franz Joseph did not like to attend balls; he was not particularly at ease with small talk and social gatherings not governed by the reassuring constraint of court etiquette. But his conscientious realization that his subjects liked him to move among them on certain well-defined occasions caused him to attend those balls where he was expected. In 1885 he was well rewarded for attending the Industrialists' Ball, one of the most brilliant occasions of the glittering Viennese carnival season. Among the guests was Katharina Schratt who, as a prominent member of the Court Theater company, was always invited to such festivities. One of the many journal keepers of the day noted that she looked particularly fetching on this occasion and that the emperor spent a considerable time chatting with her. His attraction to the vivacious star flared up again that same summer, when Katharina was part of a troupe of actors called to provide entertainment for a state visit from the emperor of Russia, Czar Alexander III. The acting was so lively and delightful that, when it ended, Franz Joseph broke all manner of court etiquette and invited the actors to dine with the royal company. It was on this occasion that Empress Elisabeth, Franz Joseph's wife, made the acquaintance of Katharina, whose name and reputation had long been known to her. And it was this evening that seems to have determined the empress to set in motion a train of events with far-reaching consequences for a number of people.

The empress Elisabeth of Austria was a striking presence. Even today, tour guides in the Imperial Palace in Vienna speak of her likes and dislikes as though she were in the next room, and this is more than a tour guide's trick. She was so beautiful, so elusive, so open in her desire to be away from court and in the company of more sensitive souls that her legend still haunts. Elisabeth's life has been told many times, from various points of view, but a few salient points are always recounted in the same way. This Bavarian princess grew up in free, happy, and quite provincial surroundings. At seventeen she was taken in marriage by her cousin, Franz Joseph of Austria, although his mother had intended for him to marry Elisabeth's sister. The young woman loved her husband, but disenchantment came early. He was away in the field a great deal; his mother systematically interposed herself between the young mother and her children; her husband did not understand her passions for delicate feelings and poetry and, although it was considered a man's need and a man's right, she, for her part, could not easily acquiesce to her husband's consorting with other women.

By the time she met Katharina, Elisabeth was already quite estranged from Vienna and the court. It was too cold, too gray, too formal, and much too connected to the concerns that had turned her dapper young military man into the nation's chief bureaucrat. The only part of her husband's domains Elisabeth could tolerate was Hungary, where she felt happy and at home. Indeed, her affection for the country and the people and theirs for her was a great factor in the negotiation of the Compromise of 1867.

When Elisabeth was not escaping to Hungary, she traveled to

Franz Joseph greeting ladies at a ball. Even as he grew older, the emperor was handsome, courtly, and pleased to speak with a lovely woman. From *Viribus Unitis* (Vienna, 1911).

England for the hunting or to Switzerland for a cure (slender and beautiful though she was, she was very concerned about her weight and her looks in general) or to Corfu to revel in her devotion to classical antiquity. Her husband, who loved her very much, suffered from her absences and always wrote to let her know how he yearned for her return. Clearly, Elisabeth felt some compunction at leaving him to his loneliness. As she made plans for being absent from Franz Joseph for even more extended periods, she seems to have decided to comfort him by finding him a suitable friend. Perhaps it is difficult to read such a statement today without a cynical smirk, but it might be worthwhile to reserve judgment and see how the story unfolded.

When Elisabeth met Katharina Schratt at the gala performance in honor of the czar of Russia and watched her husband's conversation with the actress, it must have been a clear confirmation to her that her husband found the young woman interesting and refreshing. So this, she decided, would be the one. The manner in which she then brought them together is convoluted indeed, a vivid example of court intrigue. The empress decided to have Katharina's portrait painted as a gift for the emperor, giving the commission to Heinrich von Angeli, a court painter much admired by Franz Joseph who had portrayed crowned heads, scholars, artists, and adventurers all over Europe. The order to make this portrait was brought to the artist by Ida von Ferenczy, the empress's chief lady-in-waiting, and the conditions under which it was to be done were a little difficult. The subject of the portrait was to know neither who had commissioned the portrait nor who was to receive it. Not only that, she was not even to know that the portrait would be of her. Angeli, who had a true Viennese appreciation for a complicated and amusing practical joke, accepted the challenge. He asked a colleague of Kathi's to carry a request to her. An English milord had commissioned Angeli to paint a portrait of his recently deceased wife, so that he would always have something to remember her by. Just by chance, it happened that Kathi bore an amazing resemblance to the dear departed, so could she possibly help old Angeli out and sit as the model? She said she would be delighted, and the sittings began. When the portrait was almost completed, the empress told her husband about it, and he, very eager to see this surprise, asked Angeli for permission to drop by the studio and have a preview of his gift.

At the appointed time, Franz Joseph arrived at Angeli's studio, followed closely by his wife. Delighted with the portrait, the emperor regretted the fact that the original was not there to be compared to the painting. "Your wish is my command, Majesty. She is in the next room." Katharina came in when called, not knowing in the least whom she was about to meet. The sight of the emperor and empress took her aback, and the painter had to urge her not to be frightened. She answered, "I'm not frightened, just a little scared," and once again, she was able to delight the emperor by making him laugh.

Before leaving the studio, Franz Joseph inquired politely as to Katharina's summer plans. When she replied that she had rented a villa near Bad Ischl, where he had his summer residence, he said he hoped that he would be allowed to visit her there. Then he and his wife left, and the friendship had begun. From that day until the end of her life, the empress Elisabeth protected the friendship between her husband and this lively woman, almost twenty years her junior, whom she had chosen to save her husband from unbearable loneliness. She would invite the actress to join the royal family for meals and for outings, she would send delicacies which could be prepared for the emperor in Katharina's kitchen, she asked her chief lady-in-waiting to let the two friends meet in her apartments in the palace. The message went out to anyone who kept track of such things: this woman was not a furtive figure in the shadows, to be condemned by right-thinking society, but a friend of the family.

A few days after their meeting in Angeli's studio, Franz Joseph sent the actress a note of thanks for taking the trouble to pose for the "Angelic" portrait. Enclosed with the note was an emerald ring which he begged her to accept as a memento of his gratitude. This graciousness and courtesy to a lady, this tone of courtship, marked the stream of letters and gifts that flowed to Katharina over the next thirty years. We are very fortunate to have those letters, the majority of which are preserved in the National Library of Austria; they give us a glimpse into the character of Franz Joseph, who did not hesitate to express himself to his

This portrait of Katharina Schratt was commissioned by the empress Elisabeth from court painter Heinrich von Angeli as a gift for Franz Joseph. Courtesy Austrian National Library.

friend. What he has to say is an amazing combination of the traditional Hapsburg formality, shaped by the ancient ritual of the Spanish court, and a very human interest in the goings-on of his brilliant capital city.

At first the letters were addressed to *"Meine Gnädige Frau."* There is no verbal equivalent in English to the words *"Gnädige Frau"*; the closest one could come to making such a declaration of respect and acknowledgment of position in English would be the tone of voice of a well-bred Englishman saying "Madam" to an old and eminent duchess. For want of anything better, let us say that these words mean "Gracious Lady." As the years went by and people came to see the dignity of Katharina Schratt's relationship to the imperial household and her position in Viennese society, "*die Gnädige Frau*" became the title by which other people referred to her. But Franz Joseph himself dropped it as they grew to know each other better and addressed his letters to "My dear, good friend."

These two people, so distant from each other in rank and age and origin, laid down the pattern of their meetings and visits in the summer of 1886 in the Salzkammergut, the mountainous lake region southeast of Salzburg whose salt deposits had been the rulers' personal treasure since the thirteenth century. People had been bringing salt out of the mountains there since the late Bronze Age, about 1100 B.C., and still do so today. The lakes are deep and cold, and the limestone mountains loom over them so steeply that there are places where, for some days in winter, one cannot see the sun in the sky. But in the summer, the region is delightful for vacationers, who climb mountains, sail, and savor the ancient coolness of the place.

The emperor had a summer villa in Bad Ischl, a village situated on a peninsula formed by two rivers, the Ischl and the Traun, overshadowed by mountains and surrounded by lovely, gentle walks to waterfalls and hilltops, each one with a little café for walkers to restore themselves with all manner of refreshments. At the turn of the century, this beautiful spot was a gathering place of theater people. Composers, playwrights, actors, and directors strolled and drank coffee and gossiped, while peering about to see who else was there, for these bright stars of the Viennese stage were not the only summer people. Because the emperor had a villa here, Ischl was filled with families close to the court, who moved themselves, their children, and their servants into the country for two or three months every summer. Lords and ladies doffed their city silks for Austrian peasant dress, the emperor walked among his people, unguarded, or apparently so, and the theater folk could attend to each other more than to their audiences.

For the summer of 1886, Katharina Schratt had rented a villa not far from Ischl, in the village of Frauenstein on the Wolfgangsee, without knowing that the emperor would be seeking out her company that summer. While she was still unpacking her luggage, she received a hand-delivered note dispatched by her new friend, inquiring as to the location of her house and asking whether he might come to visit in two days' time, at 8:30 in the morning. Katharina later told a friend about the excitement. There would have to be a breakfast, but it was Saturday, and the shops were already closed. The cook was told she would have to make do with what was in the house, and it was hoped that, in any case, the emperor would refuse. But he didn't. With gusto he took the first of many breakfasts in Katharina's house, at which he enjoyed the conversation, filled with gossip of Vienna, as much as the delicacies set before him. Franz Joseph, Elisabeth, and their younger daughter, Marie Valerie, visited Katharina several times that summer, sometimes all together, sometimes separately, and her friendship with the imperial household was duly noted by the world at large.

It might occur to us to wonder, as the story of the emperor and the actress unfolds, what these two people were to each other. Much ink has been spilled in speculation as to whether they were lovers, and it is quite amusing to see one and the same letter from Franz Joseph used to prove opposite sides of the argument. Whatever the truth may have been, the idea that they were not lovers produces by far the more interesting prose, as it leads to evocative descriptions of the spirit and aesthetic of the time.

Brigitte Hamann, author of an intelligently edited collection of the emperor's letters to Katharina, uses the question as a springboard for a discussion of "low" and "high" love in the late nineteenth century. To Katharina Schratt she compares Anna Nahowska, a woman who for many years was unambiguously Franz Joseph's mistress, may have borne two of his children, and certainly was elevated to the upper middle class by means of the emperor's amazingly large gifts of money, which she used for herself and her family. For the emperor's convenience, she and her husband and children were installed in an elegant villa a short walk from the summer residence, Schönbrunn Palace. For his convenience, he walked through a gate in the wall surrounding the palace grounds, crossed the street, entered the house, and soon left again. The emperor ended his relationship with Anna Nahowska in 1889, when he had already known Katharina for three years, and from the short, articulate journal she left behind we know of his former lover's pain, her fury, and her jealousy.

To this story, Hamann contrasts the comedy star in all her self-confidence, talent, and determination. It is true that she, like Anna, waited upon the emperor's pleasure and received vast sums of money from him. Indeed, she received considerably more than her predecessor. Both women were given, on a regular schedule, sufficient funds to create surroundings appropriate to the emperor's status and dignity. This included a good address and adequate furnishings as well as servants and an elegant wardrobe. At least this last was true for Katharina. (Anna was instructed by the emperor's emissary to receive His Majesty in a negligee.) However, the emperor's gifts to Katharina went far beyond that. For one thing, he frequently gave her valuable pieces of jewelry. A confidante of hers reported that once, when Katharina wanted to show a friend, Count Ferdinand of Bulgaria, her collection, she had her salon cleared out and four tables installed. On these, she sorted her jewels: one table for diamonds, one for sapphires, one for rubies, and one for emeralds. A single piece, a rather ordinary brooch, yielded enough money when it was sold in the 1930s to buy a large, luxurious city apartment and furnish it in the very finest style.

In addition to these gifts, the emperor gave his friend gifts of money for specific purposes, such as her stage wardrobe, which she had to supply herself, or to buy property or to replenish her purse after she had performed an act of particular generosity. He also provided an aristocratic education for her son, Toni, and displayed a friendly interest in his progress.

Katharina Schratt was a real person to Franz Joseph, Hamann points out, not a bundle of flesh to be bought. She engaged the emperor's imagination and held it for hours at a time with her talent for choosing an interesting topic and developing it, and when his heart was heavy, she listened to him and never breathed a word of what she had heard. She was an independent woman with a profession, or at least she would have been independent if she had not had such an unspeakably bad way with money. But most of all, she kept the emperor's respect, admiration, and eagerness by having a life of her own and never hanging her claims on him. She retained his high love by never coming too close and even letting the emperor occasionally beg for her company. But part of the pleasure and the form of their friendship was to display the appearance, the trappings, of a love affair.

The contrast of appearance and reality is presented in rather aggressive fashion by Frederick Morton in his account of Vienna's last year before World War I, *Thunder at Twilight*. Describing Franz Joseph and Katharina strolling side by side in Bad Ischl, he writes (pp. 84–85): "By 1913 they looked like a pair bonded by a passion practiced through the decades. What lay behind them instead was a quarter century of abstention. . . . In Vienna, their play unfolded invisibly: behind the garden walls of Schönbrunn Palace or over the coffee table in her breakfast room across the street from Schönbrunn. But in Ischl, the octogenarian swain and his fifty-year-old inamorata produced their romance in the open, beneath the summer sun. They simulated to perfection the trappings of a liaison."

And then Morton extrapolates from this friendship to the way the emperor ruled his country (pp. 85–86): "It was a way of love, a way of life, that came natural to Franz Joseph, the weathered centerpiece of a patinaed court. Under his reign, animation had petrified into decor. Decor—not dynamics—governed his affections as well as his politics. Both the Emperor's empire and the Emperor's affair were artifacts. Neither had much fleshly reality. Therefore, both must draw their vigor, their tang, their long lives from etiquette and accouterment. Both represented the triumph of form over substance. They were both masterpieces of survival through sheer style." This speculation is probably too extreme to be adopted as the last word on the matter, but it pro-

Katharina Schratt, no longer quite young, strolling with the emperor at Bad Ischl, where they both spent summers. Courtesy Austrian National Library.

vides a provocative reading of a remarkable story and illustrates a morality and a style quite understandable in their time.

So what was it that held these two people together—the tall, slender, courtly gentleman who had all his life regimented his own desires and feelings, and the curvaceous, lively, pretty young woman who loved to joke and gossip and wear fine clothes in fine company?

Day after day, for many, many years, Katharina Schratt gave her emperor a window on the life of his own people, as no one else understood how to do. As a popular actress, she was acquainted with all the latest stories from the life of the Second Society, and she told them with verve but without malice. She collected stories because the emperor wrote to her how much he looked forward to hearing them, and sometimes she let him know in advance that she had a good story for their next meeting. Her readiness to gossip did not go in the other direction, however. The emperor's confidante was enormously discreet in matters concerning him—she never told other people about their time together, never revealed information about the imperial family. As a result, the emperor was able to relax completely with Katharina and to speak with her about his cares and about mundane things that would have been beneath the empress's dignity to notice.

Katharina, what is more, was warm and lavishly hospitable. With the emperor's help, she had settled in a very handsome villa across the street from Schönbrunn. Its stucco walls painted the same soft yellow as the imperial residence, the villa at 9 Gloriettegasse stood in a walled garden and made a fine and prosperous impression. The regular visits of the emperor, coming as they did in addition to her life as a famous hostess, required a large staff, and so the mistress of the house employed a lady's maid, a cook, two kitchen maids, two chambermaids, a handyman, and a nursemaid for her son. In addition, she had a companion who read to her and traveled with her.

As a true-blue Viennese woman, Katharina understood the uses of food. The emperor came frequently to take meals with her, and she, cognizant of the honor, did the shopping herself at all the very best places in Vienna. One might not suppose that an emperor would consider a meal in a private house such a big treat, but he did. It was not splendor that Franz Joseph was looking for, but ordinary warmth and comfort. In the so-called smoking room of Katharina's villa, which was used only to entertain the emperor, Franz Joseph was able to make himself comfortable in his armchair and feel for a while as though he really were a good bourgeois head of household, resting after hard work and enjoying delicious smiles, delicious food, and delicious gossip. Having been protected from many realities of daily life, he was yet aware that his subjects led an existence different from his own, and in Katharina's company he had the opportunity to experience it. This extended even to very little things. The story goes, for instance, that he discovered the doorbell one day when he arrived at Katharina's house and, by some chance, there was no one waiting for him at the door. After a few puzzled moments of standing before a closed door, he noticed a button on the door frame. He pushed it experimentally and created a great ringing within. So delighted was he at this trick that he did it again and again, until the whole household came running to the door in alarm. There they found their sovereign, shaking his head with pleasure and murmuring, "What a clever arrangement!"

To a certain extent, Franz Joseph must have considered himself a part of this agreeable household, where he knew the servants' names, frequently praised the cook (about whom he wrote to his wife), and gave generous tips when he visited, as was the custom. Feeling at home, Franz Joseph came and went whenever his schedule allowed, took a meal, chatted, escorted the smiling, attentive Kathi for a stroll in his park, and brought her back to her gate like a gentleman. It is hard to tell from his letters whether he realized the strain his visits sometimes put on his friend. Possibly he knew and accepted the sacrifice as a strong token of her friendship. The emperor regularly rose at 3:30 in the morning, dressed, said his morning prayer, and went to his desk, where he started going through the waiting briefs and files. Eventually, he breakfasted and smoked a cigar. By 6:30 he was making his way through the palace park to the Gloriettegasse, where his friend would be waiting for him at the garden stairs, beautifully dressed, with every hair in place. But she, also in pur-

The emperor at his desk at the summer palace, Schönbrunn, on a normal workday. Franz Joseph was seated here, studying his agenda, considering petitions, and framing his decisions on various matters of state. He delegated as little as possible to his ministers. From *Viribus Unitis* (Vienna, 1911).

suit of her duty, had been on the stage performing until late and then, because she was usually too stimulated to sleep after a performance, reading romantic novels until 3:00 in the morning. She may have grumbled about the emperor's regimen occasionally, but clearly she never rejected it.

In the summer, Katharina entertained the emperor in Bad Ischl. In the same year that she moved into the house at the Gloriettegasse, she began to spend her summers in a house called Villa Felicitas, which was very close to the emperor's summer villa. Elisabeth gave Katharina the key to her garden gate, so that she would not have to go out into the street on her way to visit. And so the foot traffic proceeded peacefully in both directions, over a specially built bridge across the river Ischl. The early breakfasts took place here in the country, too. As always, Katharina served gugelhupf to the emperor, her own special recipe, which was baked fresh every morning. What the emperor did not know is that an identical gugelhupf—raisins, nuts, and all—was baked every day at the Konditorei Zauner, in case the one they made at home was not perfect! The emperor may have been delightfully relaxed at those morning meals, but apparently his hostess was not.

Although he did not hesitate to visit Katharina in her villa at the Gloriettegasse or her villa in Bad Ischl, the emperor did not consider it appropriate to visit her in her apartment in the inner city. He entered these rooms only once, to pay her a condolence call when her mother died. He certainly did not hesitate to invite her to the palace, where she was received in the private areas as a friend of the family. Sometimes she was entertained by the empress's chief lady-in-waiting, Ida von Ferenczy, and sometimes in the apartments of the imperial family. She would come for lunch or for tea, sometimes alone with the emperor, sometimes together with his wife, and was an accustomed guest for family dinners.

Occasionally, when Elisabeth was away and he was lonely, Franz Joseph invited Katharina to the palace for dinner. The archives of the Imperial and Royal Kitchens show that in March 1898 the emperor offered his friend:

Potage aux ravioles de vollaile	Potage with chicken ravioli
Quenelles de bécasses à la	Quenelles of woodcock à la
Diane	Diane

Pièce de boeuf et fricandeau de veau	Braised beef with fricandeau of veal
Riz de veau frit aux morilles	Fried calf sweetbreads with morels
Asperges en branches	Asparagus
Poularde rotie, salade, compote	Roast capon with salad and compote
Glaces	Ices
Champagne sec	Dry champagne
Tarte aux nois	Nut torte

Hiding in this elegant, French-sounding menu, with its early morels and asparagus, which must have been brought up from southerly parts of the emperor's domain, is the very Viennese dish Tafelspitz, masquerading as Pièce de boeuf.

Not infrequently, Katharina was invited to join the imperial family away from home. She visited them in Hungary and even on the Riviera, only there the trip was carefully choreographed in order to avoid any impression that she might be pursuing them.

But Katharina did not make the emperor so happy just by being either a delightful hostess or a delightful guest. Remarkably, in an age when women were valued for charm at least as much as for wit, for housewifeliness rather than discernment, Franz Joseph prized his dear, good friend for what she could tell him about his city and his people. She knew the artists, composers, industrialists, and diplomats who made Austria shine with a brilliant light. Her friends were able to tell her at firsthand the events, ambitions, and opinions of the day; totally unimpressed with the protocols, hierarchies, and intrigues of the court, she did not hesitate to pass on her knowledge directly to the emperor. According to many who recorded their observations, Katharina Schratt was the only person who approached him with opinions which ran counter to prevailing orthodoxies, so that her charming little stories were a strong corrective for the lies of the court camarilla. The gossip and anecdotes she collected for her meetings with Franz Joseph were a perfectly fair exchange for the gems he sent to her, and he often wrote her how much he was looking forward to the next ones.

Franz Joseph certainly did not look upon his friend as any kind of a political advisor, but there were current topics which the two discussed. For example, Franz Joseph was particularly impressed that she shared his contemptuous rejection of Dr. Karl Lueger, a charismatic, anti-Semitic xenophobe who tried several times to become mayor of Vienna before pressure overturned the emperor's opposition. Franz Joseph wrote to her, "Your views about the elections in Vienna are yet another proof of your clear-eyed, accurate political judgment. If only more people thought that way." Perhaps that is why he occasionally trusted her with extremely delicate diplomatic errands, often having to do with his own family. For example, he turned to Kathi, expecting her to enlist the help of her socialite friends, when he needed more information about his son's untimely death or when he had to prevent the publication of material that whispered scandal about his wife. He also benefited from her good relations with admirers such as the king of Bulgaria or the German ambassador.

Because Katharina enjoyed the emperor's confidence and trust, it is not surprising that she excited jealousy and enmity in very high places. Her crime was not ambition but truth-telling. As a result, there were frequent attempts to keep the emperor and the actress apart. The emperor's younger daughter, Marie Valerie, who had never approved of the friendship, was increasingly opposed to it. Once her mother was dead, she made herself the willing tool of a Jesuit priest who sought to have influence over the aging Franz Joseph. The chief chamberlain, Prince Alfred Montenuovo, was another figure hoping to separate the two old friends. He went so far as to manipulate the emperor's schedule so that he had no time to see Katharina. Although propriety was often used as a pretext for working against the friendship of Franz Joseph and Katharina, the true reason was political. Katharina, with her strong and varied connections in the liberal (industrialist, not leftist) and liberated world of the Second Society, was not attractive to the profoundly conservative aristocrats surrounding the emperor in an almost impenetrable circle. Who is to say what the outcome would have been if Franz Joseph had cultivated a more intimate contact with his country? The fact is that he did not, so that a politician loyal to the throne felt moved to write: "The mighty flow of our life and times barely reaches the ear of our Emperor as a distant thunder. He is blocked off from any real participation in this life, he no longer understands the times, and they flow over him and away."

Katharina Schratt did not only laugh and chat with the emperor, accept his presents, and send him four-leaf clovers, she also knew him well enough to console him in sorrow and stand by him when he was desolate. Franz Joseph often had occasion to lament, "I am spared nothing in this world," and he did not exaggerate by much. After the early, self-assured years of his reign, he presided over a steady decline of Hapsburg power. Military and political losses undermined the international importance of Austria, and, at home, the emperor's lack of contact with his people made for an alienating policy toward his eastern possessions. Humanly, Franz Joseph was very lonely because his early upbringing had made him leery of close contacts, and, as a ruler, he was kept in isolation by his ministers, who insulated him against all modernizing influences. His relationship with his son and heir, Crown Prince Rudolf, was poor, particularly because Rudolf's views were anti-monarchical and his social life was not of a sort to be approved of at court. But at least it was his son to whom the scepter would pass next. Or so it had always seemed. On January 30, 1889, the news came to the palace that Rudolf was dead. Elisabeth and Katharina were in the same room, waiting for Franz Joseph to stop by for a visit. When he entered, Elisabeth stepped aside, leaving it to Katharina to speak the horrible news and then to console him. The task was made more difficult by Franz Joseph's fear that his disapproval was somehow the cause of his son's suicide and by his distress at the scandalous circumstance that Rudolf's mistress had been found lying dead beside him. The double deaths were surrounded by mysteries that remain unsolved today, although Katharina did her best to obtain information from her connections among the members of

Rudolf's circle. During all the investigations, the state cere-
monies, and the ministerial consultation having to do with the
succession, Katharina's presence was heart's ease to her friend,
who wrote repeatedly that he could hardly have survived without her.

After Rudolf died, the empress spent less time than ever in
Vienna. Dressed in deep mourning, she traveled restlessly, preferring above all other places Corfu, where she had a little palace
built in the antique Greek manner. Here she picked flowers and
dreamed away her days in the world of ancient heroes, accompanied by her Greek teacher, Constantin Christomanos. Elisabeth
and Franz Joseph usually saw each other only a few weeks a year,
when they stayed at Cap Martin on the Riviera. Her absence
from court made certain kinds of rituals and festivities impossible, so that members of the First Society increasingly stayed at
home or went to their country residences. This change probably
contributed significantly to a shift of power in Viennese society.

In addition to personal tragedy and loneliness, Franz Joseph
had to struggle with political difficulties. As we have seen, he was
an extremely hardworking ruler, but his style was to fret away at
details, to read and sign every official document himself, rather
than to carry a vision. Thus, given the focus of his interest and
the isolation in which he was kept by his ministers, he was not
well positioned to confront a growing tide of national separatism
in the non-German parts of his empire, a growing shift of power
in the liberal direction.

In all of the pain and exhaustion that he felt, Franz Joseph
turned to his friend, looking forward to a letter from her or even
better, a visit, as one might long for cool water. And when the
constant dull ache which characterized most of his life turned
sharply into catastrophe again, it was probably Katharina who
helped the most to restore balance to his life. In September 1898
Elisabeth, who was by now sixty-one years old and in very poor
health, mostly from the long-term consequences of anorexia,
went to Switzerland for a health cure. While there, she made a
trip to Geneva with her lady-in-waiting, staying at a hotel under
an assumed name. Unfortunately, a Swiss newspaper discovered

Franz Joseph and his wife, Elisabeth, strolling at Cap Martin on the Riviera. Toward the end of her life, Elisabeth's rare visits with her husband tended to take place in the fragrant Mediterranean sunshine rather than at home, in a Vienna she found stiff and damp and gray. From *Viribus Unitis* (Vienna, 1911).

her identity and made it known with much excitement. This brought her to the attention of a young Italian anarchist, Luigi Lucheni, who stabbed her with a file. Seven minutes after the attack she was dead, on the deck of a steamer plying Lake Geneva.

Franz Joseph was shattered by the death of this woman whom he had loved, revered, misunderstood, and longed for most of his adult life. Katharina stood by him, visited, wrote, and was such a support to her friend that he wrote her: "God protect you and grant you health and more peace, and may he repay you for the goodness and love which you have shown me for such a long time, but especially, once more, right now, in the face of the terrible blow we have suffered. I say 'we' because in this time of sorrow, you have once more shown how very much you are one of us."

Gradually, the emperor resumed the threads of his life. A letter to Katharina, written at his Hungarian hunting lodge, Gödölő, reveals the mixture of pathos, protocol, and exercise with the gentlemen of his court that made up this life.

Gödölő, 8 November 1898

My dear good friend,

Heartfelt thanks for your telegram of the day before yesterday and for your lovely, interesting letter of the 6th which, to my great pleasure, I received yesterday at Ofen. It is truly good of you, and I am deeply touched that in spite of the continuous pressure under which you live, and the countless visitors, you tried six times to write to me and at last did manage a letter and what's more, such a long one. You are always my chief angel, at least *my* chief angel. Your worry about the growing number of visitors in your new, second floor apartment is justified, but I do hope that with time you will come to like it. I had expected that you would not like the painting by Horowitz and I can only hope that your suggestions had some effect, although I doubt it, since the task seems to me truly insurmountable. I pity the artist who spends so much effort and work on it. In Budapest, the famous Bencur is to paint a portrait of the Empress for Frau von Ferenczy and I do not doubt that there, too, nothing good will come of it. It

The first and last pages of a four-page letter to Katharina Schratt from Franz Joseph, written on mourning stationery two months after the death of the empress. Courtesy Szathmáry Collection of Culinary Arts, University of Iowa Libraries.

comforts me that your health is not altogether poor even though you are acting in many performances and have many worries, and I am very pleased that at last you were once more satisfied with a performance at the Court Theater, to the success of which you surely contributed a great deal. The day after tomorrow I will accompany you in my thoughts into the crypt and to the coffin of the dear, beloved, unforgettable one, and I will join in your prayers. I thank you from the bottom of my heart for preserving so faithfully the memory of our dear transfigured one. I am answering your dear letter today since I do have time before the hunt. Tomorrow morning, I will have to catch up with work neglected today, and early the day after tomorrow will have to travel to the city, because of audiences and cabinet ministers. The grand duchess in Gmunden appears to be near death and for that reason we will perhaps see each other soon, which would make me immensely happy. In the afternoon, the day before yesterday, at Vaalko, I'm sorry to say I only shot one young boar. Yesterday at 5:30 in the morning, I left by train for Ofen where I had only 42 audiences and was also busy with Bolfrass, who had arrived from Vienna, and several Hungarian cabinet ministers. At 3:30 I returned here with Valerie. She had traveled to town by carriage after me, and attended a requiem for the Empress at the Sacré Coeur, arranged by a number of ladies, then also visited a convent and the apartment of the Empress, where she selected Hungarian albums that are to go to the Pest National Museum. Yesterday was a beautiful, sunny, rather warm day. Tonight, with a starry sky, the thermometer stands at zero. I am afraid winter is near. Just now they brought me Hungarian cabinet papers that I have to take care of before the hunt. Therefore, adieu dearest, good, forbearing friend, kindest regards from your deeply loving

Franz Joseph

There was a dark side, too, to the relationship between Katharina and Franz Joseph, for the woman was no saint. When she was angry because the emperor would not obtain for her what she wished, she would disappear, leaving him no address to write to, sending him no pleasant, chatty letters, tearing a great hole in his already very lonely life. There is no way, nor is there any need, to judge between the two of them. Both were acting in response to their own standards and needs, and to some extent neither one understood the imperatives driving the other. There were two important things that Katharina hoped for from the emperor, and, indeed, she may even have felt that she had realistic grounds for expecting them. One was simple recognition as a firm friend of the imperial family, as a person for whom acceptance and perhaps even a bit of public recognition was a natural reward for years of closeness and availability. The recognition Katharina craved was one that the empress had promised her before her death: the Order of Elisabeth, First Class. Shortly after Elisabeth's death, Katharina reminded the emperor of the promise and asked him to grant her this honor, which was now being awarded in memory of the murdered empress. But the emperor refused. His reason was highly characteristic of his times and the rules by which he had been taught to live. Although there was ample evidence that she had performed much meritorious service for the Crown, he answered, award of the honor to her would arouse comment and raise eyebrows. As role model and father figure for his country, he was not willing to incur such scandal. This flat refusal to acknowledge the place that she had long occupied in the life of the royal family was the beginning of a very serious rift between the two old friends. The anger and disappointment Katharina felt were fatally exacerbated by the emperor's unwillingness to intervene in her disputes with the management of the Court Theater.

Over the years, Katharina had always involved herself heavily in the politics of the theater, having strong opinions about who should have power and who should not. In some cases, her wishes prevailed, partly because of her relationship with the emperor, partly because she was friendly with the management. But then the management changed and time went by, and the actress was not receiving very interesting roles or very attractive privileges any more. Of course she did not hesitate to bring this to the emperor's attention; we see from his letters that she must have been bombarding him with copious accounts of who had done what to whom. And the emperor did nothing. Whether it was out of a decent respect for the judgment of the theater's manager or a failure to understand what more Katharina could want, Franz Joseph, who made the theater possible out of his privy purse, said and did nothing to elevate the power or status of his friend. It was too much. Katharina resigned from the theater, as a ploy, being sure that she had committed a master stroke. The chief chamberlain, Montenuovo, was delighted to forward this resignation to the emperor with a straight face. Unable to see his cheerful, open friend as a tactician, Franz Joseph accepted the resignation. And so began a separation from the emperor which lasted for more than a year.

In looking at these stories from the emperor's point of view, let us remember that propriety was of utmost concern to him, since he felt absolutely obligated to demonstrate to his people how a good Christian must live. It was enough for his daughter or his cabinet minister or his confessor to tell him that an action might scandalize the people and he would abandon that action. And it was easy to make him believe that any publicly noted connection with "that actress" would arouse concern. After all, she had been the empress's friend, and that image had been zealously cultivated by all three members of the triangle. Clearly, a decent withdrawal into mourning for her departed friend was the only proper and sensitive behavior now open to Frau Schratt. While all of this was happening, the emperor wrote to the woman whom he still addressed as his dear, good, and most precious friend to reassure her that no court intrigue could deflect him from his loyal friendship and unrepayable gratitude to her. But their irreconcilable views of what constituted the behavior of a true friend made his protestation ineffectual.

Katharina traveled during her separation from the emperor and did not answer those letters and telegrams of his that managed to reach her. It was not until fifteen months later, in June 1901, that the emperor found the right words to soften her anger. He begged her, in the name of Elisabeth, whose memory was the last thing that united them, to resume their friendship. These words seem to have found Katharina's heart, and soon thereafter the emperor was invited to visit her. After a few more months of tentative pleasantness, the friendship was resumed in its old glory. From then until the emperor's death, the visits continued faithfully, at the Imperial Palace in Vienna, at the villa across the street from Schönbrunn, and, in summer, at Bad Ischl. The friends chatted and strolled arm in arm, and Katharina increasingly conferred with the emperor's valet about the old gentleman's well-being, making sure that he had warm meals when he was not presiding at state dinners. She last visited him two days before he died at the age of eighty-six in 1916. As he lay dead in his room, Katharina was recognized by the court for the last time by being allowed to come in with his family to pray for him. She laid two white roses in his hands and walked out of the room and out of the lives of the royal family.

During all the years of her friendship with the emperor, Katharina Schratt very decidedly had a life of her own. She entertained frequently, lavishly, and by all reports very well. The emperor, of course, was never present at her evening parties. Besides the fact that this kind of socializing was not at all within the bounds of the protocol prescribed for him, we must remember that many of the guests were considered undesirable by the Crown, for one reason or another. We know from his letters, however, that their doings were of burning interest to him.

Schratt was also kept preoccupied and challenged by her remarkably successful career in the theater. Unfortunately, what had started so brilliantly did not end in triumph. The declining number and importance of the roles assigned to her at the Court Theater may not have been the result of failed politics alone. It is quite possible, although not widely discussed, that Kathi's famed charm and talents were not a monument for the ages and eventually became quite out of step with the times. The Court Theater was certainly not the home of the avant-garde in Vienna, but the city was one of the hotbeds of European modernism, which may have had a diffuse, general effect on the popular taste for different pacing, a different style of humor.

After Schratt resigned from the Court Theater in October 1900, she appeared on other stages a few more times. Her last performance was the title role in the comedy entitled *Maria Theresa*; as a result, her career may not have ended in triumph, but it certainly ended in an uproar. Many, many people were simply delighted that their Kathi, even at the age of fifty, was on stage again. Others were horrified that the emperor's friend was appearing on the public stage, herself embodying one of the monarchy's most revered empresses. This objection may seem rather contrived, but perhaps one could indeed consider it a lack of discretion that the actress announced she would be wearing some of the jewels the emperor had given her. The reviews of her performance were mixed. Karl Kraus, a brilliant, bitter satirist who had never been able to stomach Schratt, characterized her behavior as the height of tastelessness, although he was not otherwise known as a defender of the dignity of the Crown. On the other hand, the dramatist and critic Hermann Bahr wrote a review of her performance which, although it hints that her day might be passing, puts a high value on her role in Viennese theater and, what is more, depicts her importance to Vienna itself:

> And this is the great secret of Schratt, who now stands equal to Girardi in the city's esteem: in her, the Viennese woman seems to see herself as she is or would really like to be, and in her, the Viennese man sees his dearest wishes fulfilled, charming and comforting. . . . One has hardly caught sight of her and already the ear is intoxicated, so amiable is this light, crisp voice, in which all the little devils of a Viennese temperament lurk, good-natured banter, cunning, and our naughty love of teasing, all ready to tumble about and burst out. But now she opens her eyes, those unbelievable eyes, distant and quiet, glittering like a far-away star, eyes of a water sprite longing for deep pools, dreamy, unearthly, remote. For these eyes, the joyously talkative mouth is really no match, the mouth that is so earthy, competent as a good housewife, energetically decisive and laughingly audacious. . . . Schratt is perhaps the last master of the Viennese art of "visiting," in which all the good ghosts of our intimate elegance are gathered one last time. . . .

When she was not in the company of Franz Joseph, Katharina was not necessarily untouchable. She had numerous admirers, some whose names we do not remember and some who were notable. There was the actor Girardi, an enormously popular figure who seems to have been somewhere between Danny Kaye and Maurice Chevalier in his appeal; the actor Viktor Kutschera, whom some call Schratt's great secret love; Ferdinand, king of Bulgaria; the heart-stoppingly attractive Hans, Count Wilczek, polar explorer, lover of art, founder of the Vienna Volunteer Rescue Corps. Others frequented her company out of sheer reciprocal enjoyment of talent—Johannes Brahms, Johann Strauss the younger, Gustav Mahler, to name only the composers. Abroad, Kathi traveled in brilliant company as well, whether on Alpine tours, gambling trips to Monte Carlo, or adventures in Egypt. The emperor knew about all her friends and all her undertakings, either from her directly or from their mutual acquaintances. Occasionally, when his friend was hard to find, he even got in touch with her lady companion to find out how she was. Of some of these figures the emperor was more jealous than others; he found the time Katharina spent with Wilczek particularly disturbing. Sometimes he tried to keep her at home by writing of his anxiety when she climbed glaciers or ascended in hot air balloons. It will come as no surprise that she rarely changed her plans.

Katharina Schratt outlived Franz Joseph by a quarter of a century and died at the age of eighty-six in 1940. In death, she was restored to propriety as the society of her heyday saw it, buried together with her husband, her son, and her daughter-in-law. She was not mentioned in the testament of the emperor which was valid at the time of his death, although it had once been his intention to grant her this public remembrance. But his rich gifts of jewels and money throughout their time together left her a prosperous woman, with a little palace on the *Ringstraße*, the great fashion spot of her youth. She lived a rather reclusive life except for warm contact with her family, giving an occasional reading for charity, working for animal welfare, entertaining a bit with great formality. And during all those quiet years, she remained discreet, never dictating her memoirs and never giving interviews about her adventures. It was as though she carried with her the noble aura of the palace where she had spent so many hours in flattering intimacy with the imperial household.

The last decades of Katharina Schratt's life seem relatively quiet and subdued, but for most of her life she was sparkling and vivid, surrounded by a convivial group and always ready for something amusing. She was a generous dispenser of delicious food and never more so than when the emperor was her guest.

Entertaining him at table was one of the most delightful ways that she could make her friend feel at home, for dining in his own palaces provided no great pleasure. The kitchens of the Imperial Palace in the center of Vienna, the Hofburg, were a vast establishment with a seven hundred–year history. Several hundred people were employed to obtain food, cook it, serve it, clear it away, polish silver, carry wood and coal to fire the voracious stoves and ovens, wash the linens, carry the food two by two in metal trunks with built-in charcoal braziers from the twelve subterranean halls where it was prepared to the upper rooms where it was served. There were meals to cook for all who served within the palace, with different menus for high and low, leftovers to be distributed to the needy, invitations to be sent, menus to be written, wines to be fetched and decanted. The records and menu files of these kitchens, over the centuries, provide a history of state visits, royal marriages, and peace congresses with a vividness not found in other state papers.

Although the menus for meals produced by the Imperial and Royal Kitchens make for succulent reading, they do not speak of comfort or of any kind of family life. What is more to the immediate point, the food itself can't have afforded the emperor much pleasure. In spite of the braziers over which food was kept as it was carried along corridors and up stairs on its way to his private apartments, Franz Joseph complained that he never got really hot food. It was probably too rich for him as well, as he was a rather abstemious man and liked very simple food best of all. Official dinners were stiff with protocol, and less formal meals, because of Elisabeth's frequent extended absences, were lonely. So it is no wonder that Katharina's offerings gave her friend great pleasure. At her house, he was served not the overwhelming French haute cuisine characteristic of the court but homey dishes she knew he liked. Two of his favorites, the spicy Hungarian meat stew called goulash and the firm, fragrant tea cake called gugelhupf, are very well represented in Katharina's kitchen notebook, together with the Transylvanian soups and roasts and game dishes enjoyed by this avid hunter.

Food for the emperor's table was transported from the kitchens to the dining room in chests with built-in charcoal braziers. This drawing, made at the summer villa in Ischl, shows how closely this process was supervised by the chef, a waiter, and a court official. From *Viribus Unitis* (Vienna, 1911).

Katharina's kitchen showed a quite different side for the elegant evening parties at which she gathered the lively company among whom she so often did diplomatic errands for the emperor. For these she would have brought out her elegant recipes, dishes named for great military and political figures, in the Victorian style, dishes very similar to those presented at court, dishes that called for shellfish brought from distant salt waters, trimmed with carefully made decorations of shimmering aspic, elaborately shaped molds, and truffles on little silver skewers.

These are the two kinds of recipes contained in the rather mysterious kitchen notebook found in the possession of Katharina Schratt's son. As a source of information, the notebook both reveals and hides. First of all, who wrote it? We know that the handwriting, quite schooled, is not that of Katharina Schratt. Most of the book seems to have been written down at one sitting—the handwriting is even and quite clear, the color of the ink and thickness of the pen do not seem to change much. In other words, it seems that the recipes in this book are being copied, not recorded one by one as they are found by the writer.

From the fact that the label on the front of the notebook bears a date, 1905, one may speculate that an orderly impulse caused the writer to review old recipes and choose what to keep for the future.

Another hint of the writer's position in the world might come from the handling of French terms. The writer knows something, but not enough. The numerous French terms in the notebook — mostly in recipe titles but sometimes in the text — are frequently spelled wrong. It seems that the ear, not the eye, decided what the French spelling would be. Was this a woman of good or at least prosperous family who was sent to finishing school in Switzerland, where German-speaking girls learned a little French but not a lot? And where did the recipes — neatly collected in this notebook, copied by an orderly woman, educated, but not too much — come from? We must listen to the notebook. Reading it, we see that this collection of recipes, belonging to a quintessentially Viennese woman, has rather few Viennese recipes in it. For instance, there is no mention of Wiener schnitzel, Semmelknödel, Tafelspitz, or of any of the delicate and delectable freshwater fish so freely available in and around the city. Rather, the two main influences seem to be Transylvanian and French! The presence of French recipes in a European cookbook with any pretensions to elegance is not very surprising. But the Transylvanian recipes might fit nicely into our story. First of all, in general things Hungarian have always fascinated the Viennese, who live so very close to the border. No matter what the political situation between the two capitals may be, and in the past it has been bad at least as often as it has been good, a desirable, exotic breeze always seems to be blowing across the flat, grassy plains from Budapest to Vienna. It would never be surprising to encounter food in Vienna served Hungarian-style.

But there is a closer connection between this notebook and Hungary. Katharina Schratt's husband, a rather ambitious man, was from Transylvania, and it was at his instigation that Katharina began to entertain, and quite lavishly, too. Could it be that he asked his mama for some suggestions? Is that where the Transylvanian foods come from, the stuffed cabbage, the white cream soups, the turkeys that were not being cooked elsewhere in Europe at this time? But what about the fact that a couple of surprising misspellings in Hungarian occur? Was the dowager Baroness Kiss so refined and westward-looking that her German was better than her Hungarian? But surely, as late as 1905 it must have been another hand that held the pen.

The really important point in trying to understand this notebook is that it is not a cookbook that just anyone can use but an *aide-mémoire* for an experienced professional cook, accustomed to managing a kitchen where there is always a ready supply of brown stock and white stock to make the great sauces of classical French cuisine, copper pans of all sizes, and a large pantry where things can be set to cool. It is a collection that indicates the variety of recipes available for fine occasions, the ingredients, more or less, that might be needed, and the effort required to prepare the dishes chosen. The reader has the impression, perhaps, of eavesdropping on a hostess who is talking to herself or to her very good cook, thinking about her next party.

Perhaps the dowager baroness Kiss did not make these notes but rather had suggested certain recipes a long time ago. Who placed the picture postcard showing the sisters of Pius X between the pages of the notebook? And where did the four-leaf clover come from? Whom and what was Toni Kiss remembering when he treasured this notebook among his effects until he died? So much speculation awakened by the evidence of this little notebook!

One thing, however, is sure. This notebook of recipes is an outstanding representation of its time and place. The food is distinctly central European and late Victorian in character. The French recipes, which bear many of the great names of classical French cuisine, frequently deviate considerably from their namesakes, both in ingredients and in methods. They seem both heavier and easier to make. There is specifically Hungarian food, and the recipes are meant to be used by someone who is so familiar with that kind of cooking that they tend to begin with a phrase like "Make a good goulash." The word paprika doesn't even occur, but that is not because no one used it but because everyone used it so much. The cuisine is certainly in the old Austrian spirit: the copious use of pork fat, the floury desserts, the interest in intricate garnishes for the good soup that had to be eaten with any self-respecting dinner. What is more, the many different recipes for dainty bites of all kinds, the decorations and garnishes suggested for entrées, the labor-intensive pureeing and straining, the use of marine shellfish hundreds of miles from the ocean, these all speak of the conspicuous consumption, far beyond the realm of comfortable plenty, that characterized the late Victorian upper bourgeoisie.

Katharina Schratt's table may have been Victorian and overly sumptuous, but it is impossible to imagine that it was ever stodgy. One can picture a table nicely set for two, with the sunlight streaming in and lovely smells wafting through the house as the actress offered her friend a late-morning bowl of goulash or an afternoon tea with cake. Or one can hear the animated conversation, the men's deep voices, the laughter of the women, the clinking of silver against exquisite porcelain as course after course is offered to a company of financiers and diplomats and artists, offered by a woman who kept the details of her friendship with Emperor Franz Joseph to herself with style and dignity as she laughed and listened and gathered up stories to tell him at their next meeting.

SOURCES

The most interesting information regarding Katharina Schratt is contained in books written in German. This is not surprising, since interest in the actress and her friendship with Emperor Franz Joseph has been more or less localized to Vienna. The present introduction hopes to make itself useful by offering in translation some of the material gathered by the German-speaking authors listed below and putting it together with what English-speaking historians have to say about this time in Vienna.

Josef Cachée. *Die Hofküche des Kaisers.* Wien-München: Amalthea-Verlag, 2d ed., 1987. A history of the kitchens in the

Imperial Palace in Vienna, with copious illustrations. Provides a view of manners and style at the imperial and royal court through the lens of food seen as an instrument of government and diplomacy. Because of its many illustrations, this book is fascinating even for readers who do not know German.

Felix Czeik. *Unbekanntes Wien 1870–1920*. Luzern und Frankfurt/M: Verlag C. J. Bucher, 1979. A photographic record of old Viennese buildings, mostly no longer standing, with an excellent essay on the political and cultural evolution of Vienna.

Brigitte Hamann. *Meine Liebe, Gute Freundin: Die Briefe Franz Josephs an Katharina Schratt*. London: Verlag Carl Ueberreuter, 1992. Much of this book consists of letters written to Katharina Schratt by Emperor Franz Joseph I over the course of thirty-two years. The letters are linked by intelligent commentary on the culture and politics of the time.

Joan Haslip. *The Emperor and the Actress*. London: Weidenfield and Nicolson, 1982. A chatty and very detailed look at the life of Katharina Schratt and her friendship with Emperor Franz Joseph I. The book is hampered by the author's unfamiliarity with the broader civilization of Austria in the period under discussion, but it does show the richness and complexity of the friendship between Katharina Schratt and Emperor Franz Joseph I.

William M. Johnston. *The Austrian Mind*. Berkeley: University of California Press, 1972. This discussion of the intellectual history of Austria gives a picture of the times of Katharina Schratt, the coming of modernism, and the changes that took place over the course of Franz Joseph's long reign.

Ann Titia Leitich. *Verklungenes Wien*. Wien: Wilhelm Andermann Verlag, 1942. This book, with its many fine photographs taken from the collection of the Museum of the City of Vienna and its reproductions of oils and watercolors, gives a picture of the comforts and glories of Vienna from the Biedermeier period to the late nineteenth century.

C. A. Macartney. *The Habsburg Empire 1780–1918*. New York: Macmillan, 1969. This scholarly history of the relationship between the rulers of Austria and the nations they ruled gives close attention to social and cultural factors.

Georg Markus. *Katharina Schratt, die heimliche Frau des Kaisers.* Wien: Amalthea-Verlag, 1982. This study briefly advances the hypothesis that some time after 1909, the emperor Franz Joseph I concluded a secret marriage of conscience with his faithful friend. Other than this unprovable claim, the book is a very valuable reconstruction of Katharina Schratt's life, based on examination of theater records, newspaper and government files, old photographs, and interviews with surviving relatives.

Frederic Morton. *Thunder at Twilight: Vienna 1913/1914*. New York: Charles Scribner's Sons, 1989. A dramatic account of the year before World War I broke out, presenting a vivid picture of society, popular arts, politics, and the reactions of the emperor in a world spinning into disaster.

Carl E. Schorske. *Fin-de-siècle Vienna: Politics and Culture*. New York: Vintage Books, 1981. Essays that interweave the artistic scene in the Vienna of the late nineteenth and early twentieth centuries with changes in political power and worldview.

Hans Tietze. *Wien: Kultur/Kunst/Geschichte*. Wien, Leipzig: Verlag Dr. Hans Epstein, 1931. An enduring work of cultural history.

Niederösterreichisches Landesmuseum. Catalog for the exhibition "Das Zeitalter Kaiser Franz Josephs." Wien: Amt der niederösterreichischen Landesregierung, 1987. This catalog gives a detailed picture of the many highly contrasting social, economic, cultural, and artistic movements existing in Austria and vying for supremacy during the second half of the nineteenth century.

🪲 COOKBOOK, 1905 🪲

Translated by Paula von Haimberger Arno

1 : *Little croustades à la Talleyrand*
Croustades filled with soufflé of partridge with salpicon of
partridge in the middle. Coat with demi-glaze sauce.

2 : *Little caisses à la Gutenberg*
Fill paper muffin cups with goose liver puree and sautéed goose
liver, top with mushrooms and demi-glaze.

3 : *Croustades with ham soufflé*
Make a pâte à choux with egg yolks, heavy cream, salt,
nutmeg, and beaten egg white. Dice ham and soaked white
marrow and fold into the batter. Fill the croustades with
this mixture and bake.

4 : *Shellfish soufflé*
Remove cooked shellfish from the shell and reserve.
Cut the shells into pieces and make a crayfish butter. Make a
good béchamel sauce with 125 g butter, 125 g flour, 1 liter
heavy cream. Season it well, let it simmer, strain, and add 125 g
crayfish butter, a pinch of paprika, 4 egg yolks, some Parmesan.
Fold in the beaten whites of 6 eggs. Arrange the pieces of
shellfish lengthwise in the glass insert of a silver casserole with
slices of truffle and a layer of béchamel sauce, sprinkle with
Parmesan cheese, and bake slowly for 1-1/2 hours.

5 : *Crayfish mousse*
Cook 40 crayfish and remove the meat from the shell.
Reserve the best-looking tails and claws from 20 crayfish as
garnish. Mince and puree the rest. Prepare a thick, well-cooked
white sauce and add the crayfish puree, a piece of crayfish butter

as big as an egg, cayenne pepper, and a pint of heavy cream. Grease a copper mold with almond oil, pour in the mixture, and let it rest, covered with ice, for three hours. Turn the mousse out onto a platter and garnish it with the reserved pieces of crayfish and aspic.

6 : *Little croustades à la Dauphine*
Fill croustades with a mixture of forcemeat quenelles, diced truffles, and a fine white sauce.

7 : *Patty shells à la Dauphine*
The same, but use patty shells instead of croustades.

8 : *Little patty shells à la Joinville*
Fill with julienne and salpicon.

9 : *Crayfish crépinettes*
Wrap a salpicon of crayfish in caul. Cover with egg and crumbs and fry. Serve very hot.

10 : *Little plover nests*
Fill little cases made of forcemeat with a puree of game, top with plover eggs and glaze.

11 : *Little timbales à l'Agnès Sorel*
Fill forcemeat timbales with salpicon, make a small depression in each one, top with plover eggs and glaze.

12 : *Croquettes à la diplomate*
Form well-shaped croquettes of goose liver, truffles, mushrooms, chicken, and veal, cover with bread crumbs, and fry until golden brown.

13 : *Little croustades à la Strassbourg*
With goose liver puree, decorated with sautéed goose liver and covered with demi-glaze.

14 : *Little croustades Cap de Cougère*
Fill with salpicon of wood grouse.

15 : *Little quail timbales Périgord*
Fill forcemeat timbales with salpicon of quail, cover with
truffle sauce.

16 : *Little bouchées à l'impériale*
Fill with truffles and julienne and cover with madeira sauce.

17 : *Short dough for croustades*
On a board, work 125 g flour, 100 g butter, a little salt, and
1 egg yolk into a dough. Moisten dough with wine and work
until it forms air pockets.

18 : *Croquettes à la russe*
Dip white croquettes of salpicon into frying batter and fry them
in hot lard.

19 : *Little croustades à la Colbert*
With chicken puree and plover eggs.

20 : *Plover eggs à la Rohan*
Croustade with champignon puree and plover eggs.

21 : *Timbale of plover eggs*
Forcemeat timbales and plover eggs.

22 : *Little croustades à la Dauphine*
With champignon puree and a chicken cream.

23 : *Little pastry cases filled with veal sweetbreads*
Add coarsely cut sweetbreads and champignons to a white
ragout sauce and pour into pastry cases. Sprinkle with cheese
and white bread crumbs and bake.

24 : *Little timbales à l'impériale*
Add truffles and asparagus tips to a white sauce, pour into croustades, and garnish with plover eggs.

25 : *How to cook goose liver*
Cook the liver in wine with a little water and salt for three minutes and allow it to rest in this broth overnight. It can be used for various recipes, for instance, ragout of goose liver or croustades. It can also be covered with aspic or used in patty shells, etc.

26 : *Game pudding*
Mince 250 g rabbit or similar meat and 67 g bacon, add half a roll with crust trimmed off, soaked in milk, and salt. Stir in thoroughly one egg and one yolk. Add some diced truffle. Pour the mixture into a well-oiled pudding mold and steam it. Coat the pudding with a fine game sauce and garnish with croutons.

27 : *Rice sausages*
Cook rice in milk, salt it, and allow it to cool. Form little sausages out of the rice, then bread and fry them.

28 : *Cheese soufflé*
Put 33 g flour into a saucepan, stir in 175 ml heavy cream, 1 whole egg, 1 yolk, and 50 g butter. Stir this dough over heat until it forms a ball, place it in a bowl, stir in 2 yolks, stir the dough until it is cold. Add 35 g Parmesan and 4 beaten egg whites.

29 : *Hodge-podge*
Oil a bowl and coat it with crumbs. Cover it with a layer of very thin potato slices, then layers of minced veal, ham, anchovies, and sardines, sliced eggs and frankfurter sausages. Beat egg and cream together and pour over the layer, together with some melted butter. Alternate these layers until the casserole is full, then sprinkle the top with grated Parmesan cheese.

30 : *Rissoles à la russe*

Cut ham fairly fine, make a roux, add the ham, pour cream and a little pepper over it, cool the mixture. Cut rectangles of puff pastry with a pastry wheel, fill them with the mixture, roll them up, and bake.

31 : *Mixed seafood dish*

Cook a lobster and remove the meat from the shell. Lay the meat into the center of a bowl, surround it with breaded, fried filets of sole, bread crumb dumplings, quenelles of minced fish, garnish with whole cooked champignons, truffles, and hollandaise sauce. Additional sauce is served on the side.

32 : *Fritto-misto*

Dip into flour and egg: lobster, fresh sardines, sole, sweetbreads, cauliflower, shrimp, and oysters. Fry in fine oil. Fry parsley as well. Mix all the fried pieces together on a platter. Serve with remoulade sauce.

33 : *Goose liver patty shells*

Line round forms with short dough, fill them with dried peas, cover with a circle of dough, and bake. Sauté boiled goose liver in butter and cut it into small cubes. Make a roux, add some meat glaze, lemon juice, and finely sliced truffles. Remove covers and dried peas from pastry shells, fill the shells with the goose liver mixture, and replace the covers.

34 : *Stuffed bread*

Beat 200 g butter until fluffy. Mince finely 100 g ham, 100 g tongue, 2 hard-boiled eggs, 5 anchovies, a rounded teaspoon capers. Add mustard and mix all this with the beaten butter. Scoop out a good-quality ten-penny loaf and fill with the mixture. Store in a cold place, then serve sliced.

35 : *Chicken casserole*

Steam rice. Boil a chicken wrapped in bacon in a good soup with soup greens. Place the rice in a casserole, then the skinned

and carved chicken pieces. Add slices of goose liver, truffles, and
mushrooms. Cover with a well-seasoned white sauce.
Serve very hot with more sauce on the side.

36 : *Lenten risotto with eggs*
Prepare a mushroom risotto. Boil eggs, not too hard, and add
to risotto before serving.

37 : *Rabbit bread*
Line a loaf mold with a short dough. Prepare a stuffing of
ground rabbit thigh meat, bacon, pâté spices, and a bit of thick
brown savory sauce. Spread this over the dough in the pan.
Place slices of larded rabbit filet into the pan, then add more of
the stuffing and fold over the dough. Bake for two hours. When
done, pour liquified aspic into the loaf. When the aspic is well
set, take the dish out of the pan and cut nice slices.

38 : *Pheasant pâté*
Bone a roast pheasant breast, rub it with salt and pâté spices,
and set aside. With the rest of the meat and some bacon,
prepare a forcemeat. Boil the giblets, liver, neck, and wing tips
in water with some soup until the liquid is well reduced; add
this to some sauce espagnole. Add the sauce to the forcemeat
and season with salt, pepper, and pâté spices. Line a terrine with
bacon, cover with forcemeat, place the well-larded breast pieces
in the center. Cover with more forcemeat and bacon. Steam
for three hours. Set terrine on ice and serve cold.

39 : *Cabbage dumplings*
Prepare a forcemeat of pork, 1 egg, and raw rice. Cut the ribs
out of some nice cabbage leaves and scald the leaves. Wrap the
stuffing in the leaves and tie. Cook the dumplings together with
sauerkraut and some paprika until done. Remove the dumplings
and with the remaining liquid make a thin roux, add some
sour cream, and replace the dumplings, with threads
removed, in the sauce and serve.

40 : *Jellied goose*

Cut up a meaty goose that is not too fat. Remove excess fat. Boil the goose with pepper, bay leaf, salt, vinegar, allspice, and four veal knuckles. Take out the breast before the rest of the meat so that it does not get too soft. Slice all the meat into nice helpings and place into a porcelain dish. Continue boiling the jelly until the knuckles are well done. Taste the jelly for seasoning; if necessary, add a little wine, salt, and vinegar, then clarify with egg white. Pour the jelly over the slices of goose, place the dish on ice until jelly is firm.

41 : *Omelette St. Hubert*

Omelette filled with game puree.

42 : *Stuffed potatoes*

On a baking sheet, bake very large potatoes in the oven. Scoop out the potatoes but leave a wall and keep a cover attached so as to form a box. Before serving, stuff the potatoes with the following filling: prawns with crayfish sauce (if prawns are not available, pieces of crayfish), top with a peeled three-minute egg, also a slice of truffle that wedges the potato cover open. Place the potatoes on napkins and serve.

43 : *Mutton chops*

Roll up boneless mutton chops, place them on silver skewers, and grill them.

44 : *Eggs à la Rossini*

Poached eggs, croutons, goose liver puree, truffle, and madeira sauce.

45 : *Eggs à l'américaine*

Poached eggs and ham on croutons, covered with a tomato sauce.

46 : *Eggs à la Nelson*

Poached eggs with ham, champignon puree, salpicon, and truffles on toast.

47 : *Eggs à la Mazarin*

Poached eggs, half rounds of toast covered with goose liver, tongue, demi-glaze.

48 : *Eggs à l'impériale*

Poached eggs with goose liver puree and madeira sauce.

49 : *Eggs à l'opéra*

Scoop out fresh tomatoes, surround them with paper strips, and sauté them lightly in butter. Place an egg in the center of each one and cover with demi-glaze.

50 : *Eggs à la reine*

Poached eggs on toast, covered with chicken puree and truffles.

51 : *Eggs à la Meyerbeer*

Roast two kidneys on a spit. Place them in a buttered pan, break a small egg over the center of each kidney, and finish cooking. Cover with tomato sauce and aspic.

52 : *Omelette à la Gutenberg*

Fill with goose liver puree.

53 : *Omelette à la reine*

Fill with pureed chicken.

54 : *Omelette with lobster*

Fill with lobster pieces sautéed in butter.

55 : *Omelette à la portugaise*

Place pieces of tomato sautéed in butter under the omelette.

56 : *Omelette à la provençale*
The same as omelette portugaise, but add slices of fried sausage.

57 : *Potage royale*
Bouillon with colored forcemeat quenelles and chervil.

58 : *Crème royale soup*
White chicken puree garnished with cutouts of colored
forcemeat.

59 : *Cockscomb soup*
To a bouillon add madeira, cockscombs cut into strips,
forcemeat soufflé, and truffles.

60 : *Camerani soup*
Mix well a sautéed julienne of vegetables, macaroni,
boiled chicken, and grated Parmesan. Place in a casserole
lined with butter and bread crumbs and bake.
Moisten with bouillon.

61 : *Soup à la Rohan*
Bouillon garnished with designs cut out of celery root, carrots,
peas, and chervil. Serve with toast spread with game forcemeat.

62 : *Duchess soup*
A bouillon with small meatballs.

63 : *Turtle soup à l'anglaise*
Cook partridges in a strong bouillon. Add madeira, juice of a
meat roast, turtle meat, and a calf's head. Forcemeat quenelles
and turtle dumplings are placed in the soup.

64 : *Partridge garnish à la France*
Julienne crosscut into tiny cubes with truffles and pieces
of partridge.

65 : *Soup à la Rochelle*
Bouillon garnished with designs cut out of artichoke bottoms, asparagus tips, and decorated forcemeat quenelles.

66 : *Soup à la Pierre le Grand*
Brown champignon puree soup with forcemeat quenelles.

67 : *Soup à l'Orléans*
Consommé with white and red forcemeat quenelles, peas, and rice.

68 : *Harlequin soup*
Consommé with red, white, green, and multi-colored forcemeat mousselines with chervil.

69 : *Consommé à l'impériale*
Clear consommé, round forcemeat quenelles, artichokes, cock kidneys, peas, and chervil.

70 : *Soup with salpicon ravioli*
Clear bouillon with extra-small ravioli filled with forcemeat and salpicon.

71 : *Soup à la chantilly*
Brown game puree with lentils, madeira, forcemeat quenelles, julienne, game sausages, and some heavy cream.

72 : *Puree of mountain-cock soup*
Mountain-cock puree with asparagus tips and croutons.

73 : *Soup à l'Artoise*
Barley porridge with julienne, sorrel, and croutons.

74 : *Soup à la Poligny*
Chicken puree soup and chicken cream soup mixed with truffles, tender peas, beans, and asparagus tips.

75 : *Soup à la Montpensier*
White ragout soup, round forcemeat dumplings, and
steamed rice.

76 : *Soup à la Xavier*
Bouillon, puree of peas royale, chicken blanquette, and chervil.

77 : *Hors d'oeuvre*
Soft-boil and peel plover or other eggs. Over each egg
place a cross of blanched tarragon. Add chopped tarragon to an
aspic. Place the eggs on aspic in a serving dish and pour
over them enough aspic to cover. When set,
serve in the same dish.

78 : *Lenten dish*
Slice boiled potatoes thin and fry them in butter,
without breaking them, until they have a nice crust. Mix pieces
of crayfish, lobster, or mushrooms with some sour cream
just before serving. Place in a round dish, cover with
potatoes, crust-side up, and top with fried eggs.

79 : *A good appetizer*
Fried bratwurst is thinly sliced at a slant and layered
on individual plates with tomato puree and fried eggs.
(First tomato puree, then two slices of sausage,
then one egg; repeat.)

80 : *Hors d'oeuvre*
Hard-boiled eggs are halved lengthwise. The rounded
underside is trimmed so that the egg will stand. With a pastry
bag form a wreath of anchovy butter around the yolks. In the
center place a teaspoon of caviar. Decorate with parsley.

81 : *Four kinds of breakfast butter*
One small loaf is spread with truffle butter, one with herb
butter, one with anchovy butter, and one with plain butter.

82 : *Fine sandwiches*

Pass butter and goose liver through a sieve. Stir finely
chopped eel, one sardine, one anchovy, mustard, paprika, lemon
juice, and lastly caviar into the butter mixture. Spread on
slices of toasted roll.

83 : *Swabian Spätzle*

Mix 2 cups flour, two eggs, salt, and water into a dough.
Beat thoroughly until the dough becomes elastic. Roll it on a
board and cut long, narrow strips (like egg noodles). Cook the
strips in boiling water. Each time the board is empty and
quantities of the spätzle have been cooked, remove
them to a serving bowl. Cover them with butter
and bread crumbs. They can also be
lightly pan fried.

84 : *Fish baveuses*

Slice white bread, remove the crusts. Between two slices
spread the following stuffing: finely chopped raw sole, plenty of
minced champignons sautéed in butter with parsley, a bit of
lemon juice, one or two rolls softened in milk, salt, cayenne
pepper, Worcestershire sauce, and sautéed onions. Thin leftover
filling with fish broth and spread on the serving dish. The
stuffed bread slices are dipped in milk and egg and fried.
Place them on top of the thinned filling.

85 : *Lenten appetizer*

Tomato rice is served with anchovies and herring that have
first been soaked in milk to remove the acid, then breaded with
egg and bread crumbs and fried.

86 : *Duckling à la voisine*

Roast two young ducklings and place them on ice.
Prepare a forcemeat of the livers and a few chicken livers, bacon,
and spices. Set it aside in a cool place. Bone one of the ducks
and set aside. Prepare a tasty sauce from the carcass, flavored

with madeira aspic and brown sauce. Then grind the duck, add the liver forcemeat, then the good sauce. Rub this puree through a hair sieve and adjust the seasoning. Fill the cleaned cavity of the other duck with the puree. Set on ice. Serve cold, decorated with madeira aspic.

87 : *Savoy cabbage, Hamburg style*
Strip the cabbage from the stems, wash, and set to boil with smoked meat. Prepare a white sauce with the cooking liquid. Place the savoy cabbage in the sauce, season with pepper, and briefly bring to a boil. The cabbage is usually served with Hamburg-style smoked meat.

88 : *Game pudding*
Grind 250 g rabbit or deer meat with 67 g bacon.
Add one roll softened in milk, salt, pepper, and pâté spice, one whole egg, one yolk; mix well, then add cubed truffles and champignons. Steam the pudding, decorate it with croutons, and serve with game sauce.

89 : *Capon trifle*
One liter light cream, six tbs. flour, six yolks, six beaten egg whites, sugar, salt. First whisk part of the cream with the yolks and the flour, then add the rest of the cream. Lightly mix in the beaten egg whites. In a large pan, melt butter and a bit of beef fat. Pour in the batter and brown lightly, tear into strips with two forks, and turn strips to brown on both sides. Carve a nicely roasted capon, take the meat off the bones, and cut into a fairly coarse hash. Place some of the omelette strips in a serving dish, then the meat hash, then omelette strips and some pan juice from the roasted capon.

90 : *Fish croquettes*
Grind raw fish. Add onion and parsley sautéed in butter, salt, and pepper, and form croquettes. Decorate the croquettes nicely and bake.

91 : *Hamburg salad*

Mix finely sliced roast veal, small gherkins, and beets with a little vinegar and a generous quantity of oil. Top off the dish with a star formed of all the ingredients.

92 : *Japanese goulash*

Cut the breast of a goose into small cubes and sauté it in butter; add salt and dust the meat lightly with flour. Add meat glaze and soup.

93 : *Goose liver ragout*

Cut the goose liver into slices and fry it. To prepare a good sauce, make a roux of clarified butter, flour, reduced stock, and madeira; add sliced truffles and continue cooking. Arrange the goose liver in a mound on a serving dish, surround it with forcemeat quenelles, and pour the sauce over it.

94 : *Forcemeat quenelles*

Put 300 g of nice veal through a meat grinder at least three times. Stir and sauté some softened white bread, without crusts, 2 eggs, and butter until the mixture looks like scrambled eggs. After it has cooled, mix with the meat, add salt and nutmeg, and pass it through a sieve. Then add one yolk and a little milk and form nice quenelles.

95 : *Semolina soup garnish*

Cook 200 g semolina in 700 ml milk. Cream 167 g butter, add slowly 15 egg yolks and last, the beaten egg whites. Steam this mixture.

96 : *Leg of mutton à la Strasbourg*

Serve braised leg of mutton in its own juice, to which sliced champignons and small gherkins have been added.

97 : *Mutton cutlets à la Nelson*

The cutlets are salted, seasoned with pepper, quickly browned, and then lightly braised in meat juice in charlotte molds. When serving, sprinkle with grated Parmesan.

98 : *Goose liver pudding*

Have ready goose liver and also some calf's liver. Prepare forcemeat from veal and pork fat as for goose liver pâté and pass through a sieve. Add truffles to the liver. In an oblong dish, make layers of forcemeat, then liver and truffles, then forcemeat. There can be more forcemeat than liver. Steam the pudding. The dish can be served warm, with truffle sauce (in which case it should be prepared in a ring mold), or cold, with aspic.

99 : *Goose liver pâté*

Place a nice white goose liver in cold water to which milk has been added. Let it soak for a whole day. Change the liquid frequently so that the liver becomes nice and white. Cut ample slices from the liver, remove the skin, cover the liver slices with truffles, salt, and pâté spices. Prepare the following forcemeat: For six pieces of nice liver, take 560 g nice white veal, 320 g pork belly, one large roll softened in milk. When the veal is finely ground, add the pork fat, the roll, and goose liver scraps. Mash all the ingredients together and pass the mixture through a sieve. Place it in a bowl and beat it well until it is nice and white, then add pâté spices, salt, pepper, rum, and madeira. Line a terrine with bacon, fill it with layers of forcemeat and liver until the terrine is full. Top with lard, then cover tightly with paper, to prevent steam from entering. Steam the pâté for 3 hours, do not remove it until the next day. Press the pâté to make the fat rise. Discard the juice. Put the well-covered pâté on ice for 8 days. Then scoop out pâté with a heated tablespoon and serve it nicely decorated with aspic.

100 : *Turbot filet à l'ostendaise*
On a serving platter, form a border of fish forcemeat.
Cut nice filets of turbot and sauté them. Arrange the filets
pleasingly on the platter. In the center, place green and white
forcemeat dumplings, champignons, oysters, and
steamed mussels. Cover with a good white sauce
and serve with potatoes.

101 : *Filet of sole à l'américaine*
Sauté filets of sole, folded in half, with a little paprika. On a
serving dish fashion a border of fish forcemeat, arrange the filets
pleasingly, add forcemeat quenelles, place on each filet a fluted
champignon and in the center a row of lobster pieces. Garnish
with potato rounds and pour sauce américaine over the
assembled dish or serve the sauce on the side. Sauce américaine
preparation: a brown, very piquant sauce with white wine.
Before serving, add finely chopped parsley.

102 : *Soup garnish à la royale*
Thoroughly whisk 7 yolks with 250 ml very fine poultry soup,
add salt and nutmeg. Pass this through a fine sieve. Steam the
mixture in a buttered mold. When done, cut into cubes and
serve in the bouillon.

103 : *Egg garnish*
Melt 375 g butter in a casserole, add 375 g flour, simmer
briefly, stir in 500 ml boiling milk, and whisk until the mixture
leaves the sides of the casserole. After it has cooled, mix with
14 egg yolks, a little salt, and fold in 10 beaten egg whites.
Steam for one hour, slice, and serve in the consommé.

104 : *Sauce à la Suvorov*
Whisk 10 egg yolks with a cup of tarragon vinegar over
warm water until thickened. Then beat in a generous quantity
of melted butter, some meat glaze and meat juice, and finally
caviar. The sauce is to be treated like béarnaise and goes
with rump steak, filet, roast beef, and similar dishes.

105 : *Patty shells à la Savarin*

Make four fairly large patty shells. Prepare a fine ragout by cutting chicken breasts, cocks' combs, truffles, champignons, cauliflower into small pieces. Add small forcemeat quenelles and crayfish. Fill the patty shells and bake.

106 : *Strasbourg pâté*

Soak nice goose liver in water mixed with milk, lard the best pieces with truffles, and pass the rest through a sieve. Melt good belly lard and sauté an onion in it. Pass it through a sieve, then add 2 rolls softened in milk. Add fine spices, madeira, and rum to this mixture and put it on ice to set. Line molds with the forcemeat, add liver, repeat until molds are filled; cover them well with paper and steam them.

107 : *Garnish for chicken soup*

Melt butter, add onions and let them steam; make a roux with white flour; add milk and cook until thick. Chop roast veal, add it to the sauce, and puree. Add 2 eggs and 4 yolks. Steam.

108 : *Champignon garnish*

Steam champignons in butter. Dust them with 3 tbs. flour and let them brown. Add soup and cook until the sauce thickens. Puree the sauce, add salt, stir in 10 yolks, and steam.

109 : *Parmesan egg garnish*

Beat the whites of 10 eggs, add a scoop of flour, 250 g grated Parmesan, 10 yolks, and a bit of melted butter and salt. Bake.

110 : *Genoa sauce*

Mix anchovy butter with white and brown sauce and a bit of beaten egg white.

111 : *Fillet à la Trauttmansdorff*

Roast a beef tenderloin just until rare. Place chicken risotto in the center of an oval serving platter and pieces of filet along each side. Pour juice from the roast over the dish.

112 : *Stephanie roast*

Trim a piece of beef nicely, then cut holes in the meat with a knife. Place hard-boiled eggs in the holes close enough to touch each other. Salt and pepper the roast, put it in a pan with soup greens and spices, and braise it in the oven. Add a roux, or dust with flour and baste with beef stock. Sour cream, lemon juice, and a bit of red wine will give the sauce a piquant flavor.

113 : *Fillet à la Walter Scott*

Wrapped in a good potato dough, roasted rare, and glazed with butter.

114 : *Rumpsteak à la princesse*

Decorate with a small rose fashioned from anchovy butter.

115 : *Beef steak fillets à la Pálffy*

The steaks are browned and lightly dusted with flour. Tomatoes, diced cucumbers, and potatoes are added and all this is braised. Chopped parsley is added before serving.

116 : *Fillets à la duchesse*

Add champignons and hard-boiled eggs to sautéed fillets.

117 : *Gypsy roast*

Braise a good cut of beef until done, prepare a well-browned sauce, add a little red wine, and before serving add thinly sliced potatoes.

118 : *Goulash à la Debrecen*

Cook a very good beef goulash. When it is partly braised, add soup greens, cut into small cubes. To serve, garnish with small pickles cut lengthwise.

119 : *Cowboy's meat*

Braise beef goulash until partly done. Then add one part pork, one part veal. When done, dust with flour and add broth.

122. Andrassy Gulyass.

123. Seccelie - Gulyass.

124. Hollstein - Gulyass.

125. Reindl - Gulyass.

126. Stefanie - Gulyass.

127. Pastetchen à la reine.

This page from "Cookbook, 1905," shows just a few of the many goulash recipes presented. It also illustrates the writer's idiosyncratic spelling of both Hungarian and German. Courtesy Szathmáry Collection of Culinary Arts, University of Iowa Libraries.

120 : *Gypsy goulash*

From beef, pork, and veal, prepare a good goulash, add raw potatoes. Serve with sliced small pickles.

121 : *Goulash à la Troppau*

This is a good beef goulash served with baked marrow dumplings.

122 : *Goulash à la Andrássy*

This is also a good beef goulash, with anchovies and broad noodles.

123 : *Goulash à la Székely*

The sauce as above, but with sauerkraut and topped with green peas.

124 : *Goulash à la Holstein*

To the goulash add diced cucumbers and a fried egg.

125 : *Kettle goulash*

To the goulash add potato rounds and a fried egg.

126 : *Goulash à la Stephanie*

Add spinach dumplings.

127 : *Patty shells à la reine*

Prepare a finely chopped chicken hash. In a casserole, melt butter over low heat, add finely chopped parsley and the chicken hash, a bit of madeira, lemon juice, a thick, fine butter sauce, a few yolks, the necessary salt and nutmeg. The hash must be thoroughly thickened. Pour it into puff pastry shells. Put the pastry cover over the shells and serve with some of the thickened butter sauce.

128 : *Chicken hash croquettes*

These are prepared as above but instead of yolks, whole eggs and bread crumbs are used to thicken the mixture. Let it cool, spread it on a board, and form croquettes. Coat them in egg and bread crumbs and fry until golden brown.

129 : *Chicken rissoles*

Use the chicken hash from the preceding recipe but let it cool completely. Fashion rissoles from a puff pastry or short dough, fill them, and deep fry. Serve the rissoles with

a fine green vegetable. (The chicken croquettes can also be
served this way.) They also can be served
with scrambled eggs.

130 : *Omelette with chicken hash*
Prepare a good egg omelette and fill it with soft chicken hash.

131 : *Chicken hash with egg*
A well-prepared, fairly soft chicken hash is placed in a
scallop shell or casserole. Top it with a fried egg. In place of
the egg, puff pastry crescents or croutons may be used.
All the chicken hash dishes listed can be prepared
just as well with veal hash.

132 : *Ragout in patty shells*
Take sweetbreads, veal, smoked tongue, a good cut of
beef, truffles, and champignons, cut into small cubes and pass
through a sieve. Add madeira and pour into patty shells.
Pour a thickened butter sauce around the shells.

133 : *Omelette with salpicon*
Make a good egg omelette and fill with salpicon.

134 : *Patty shell with venison hash*
Grind fine roasted venison, add madeira and some piquant game
sauce. Pass through a sieve and fill the patty shells. Surround the
shells with fine venison sauce. One can prepare all the above
chicken and veal dishes with the venison hash.

135 : *Poultry rice with Parmesan*
Steam rice, then boil poultry, including gizzard and liver.
Cut the meat into small pieces, add a bit of lemon juice and
nutmeg. Meanwhile, prepare a good white sauce with the
poultry soup, thicken the sauce, and add a little to the meat.
Butter a mold, put into it a layer of rice, then a layer of
the meat, then another layer of rice. Turn out onto a

serving dish, surround with sauce, and top with Parmesan.
In place of Parmesan, finely chopped ham can be used.
In that case the dish is called Rice à la turque.

136 : *Risibisi with poultry*
Prepared as in the above recipe, but tender young peas and
Parmesan are added. Before serving, add more Parmesan.

137 : *Poultry rice cardinal*
Prepare a good tomato rice. Fill with poultry pieces and
surround with tomato sauce.

138 : *Poultry rice sailor's style*
Steam rice. Instead of plain butter, add a fairly large piece
of crayfish butter. Boil poultry, then add to it crayfish tails and
claws. Butter a mold and place a layer of rice on the bottom,
the small ragout in the middle, then another layer of rice.
Turn the mold out onto a serving dish and pour over it
a sauce thickened with crayfish butter.

139 : *Hungarian stuffed cabbage*
Remove the core from a head of cabbage. Blanch the
cabbage. Prepare a fine forcemeat of lean pork, lightly sautéed
onion and parsley, salt, a few eggs, some white pepper, and
steamed rice. Then take cabbage leaves, remove the ribs and fill
the leaves with forcemeat. Roll them up, but not too tightly.
Place a layer, about a finger thick, of sauerkraut, slightly
thickened with a roux, into a roasting pan. Add the
cabbage rolls, a bit of sour cream, paprika, and
bread crumbs, also a few strips of bacon, and
bake in the oven until golden. Serve the
cabbage rolls with the sauerkraut.

140 : *Stuffed tomatoes*
Slice nice large tomatoes in half horizontally, remove the
seeds. Fill one half with fine veal forcemeat and some less finely
ground veal hash to make the stuffing less solid. Cover with

the other half. Place the stuffed tomatoes in a buttered pan
to which a bit of soup has been added and bake them
in the oven. They may be served as a small appetizer
or as garnish for fillets or braised beef.

141 : *Chicken ragout à la Pompadour*
Prepare a fine chicken ragout. Prepare a fine forcemeat and
steam in a ring mold. Invert the mold onto a serving plate. Place
chicken breasts on top and decorate them with stars cut out of
truffles and stuck on with egg white. Fill the center of the ring
with the ragout and some cauliflower. Border the plate with
nice pastry crescents and place in the center of the dish a
silver skewer with a whole truffle, one champignon, and
a puff pastry ball decorated with a pastry crescent or a
Maltese cross. Serve with a fine, thickened sauce.

142 : *Stuffed turkey à la Périgord*
Take a turkey hen that is not too large, singe, clean, and wash.
Loosen the breast skin without tearing it to form a pocket, just
as is done with pigeons and roasting chickens. The breast
cannot be washed from then on. Prepare a fine veal forcemeat
with madeira and a lot of thinly sliced truffles. Beat the
forcemeat well and fill the breast with it. Tightly tie the
neck opening. Place the turkey on its back and roast it,
starting with a moderate oven. Cover the roast with paper
to avoid tearing the skin, baste frequently with butter.
Carve the turkey nicely and serve it with the
thoroughly defatted sauce.

143 : *Brain croquettes*
Sauté chopped parsley in butter and add the calf's brains after
the outer membranes have been removed. Cut up the brains,
add salt and a bit of white pepper, butter sauce, and an egg.
Thicken the mixture with bread crumbs and let it cool.
On a board, form croquettes, bread them with egg and
bread crumbs, and fry until nice and golden.

144 : *Baveuses filled with brains*

Remove the crust from white bread and cut into finger-thick slices. Spread the sautéed brains, prepared as in the preceding recipe, thickly between two slices of bread. Dip the slices in cold milk, lightly beaten eggs, and bread crumbs, and quickly fry in hot, deep fat until golden yellow. Serve with spinach, kale, or other green vegetables.

145 : *Omelette with brains*

Prepare a soft egg omelette and fill it with lightly sautéed brains.

146 : *Patty shells with brains*

Sauté brains, add some butter sauce and eggs, salt, and pepper. Fill the patty shells with this mixture and pour a light butter sauce over them.

🐚 DESSERTS 🐚

1 : *Chilled iced cream*

To 500 ml whipped cream add 135 g vanilla sugar. Depending on your preference, use pulp of strawberries, raspberries, currants, or chocolate, almonds, praline, hazelnut, coffee, etc., to flavor the following cream: 350 ml heavy cream, one cup milk, 3 yolks, 67 g sugar are whisked over heat until thick. After the mixture has cooled, fold it into the whipped cream and pour it into an ice cream mold. Set the mold into crushed ice. Use 5 kg ice to 1 kg salt.

2 : *Almond crescents*

Beat 4 egg whites until stiff, blend in 234 g sugar, 234 g blanched almonds coarsely chopped. Spread on a board, form crescents, and roll them in chopped almonds. Bake on a well-buttered cookie sheet in a cool oven.

3 : *Coupe Jacques*

Cut fruit such as peeled melon, pineapple, peaches, apricots, plums, into bite-sized cubes; use also currants, strawberries, grapes. Peel where indicated. Soak the fruit in kirsch and maraschino and set aside on ice until ready to use. Prepare a very firm strawberry ice. To serve, fill champagne glasses half full with the fruit, cover with the strawberry ice, and smooth the surface. In the center, place one green grape and around it four blanched almond halves to make the arrangment look like a flower. Serve with small cookies. This is a dessert suitable for an elegant dinner.

4 : *Sugar syrup for fruit ices*

Clarify sugar by boiling 500 g sugar and 350 ml water and skimming off the foam.

5 : *Lemon ice*

Combine the juice of three lemons, some essence of lemon, 700 ml clarified sugar, 700 ml water. The mixture must measure 18 degrees on the sugar scale. If it weighs more, add water; if it weighs less, add sugar. Before freezing, add the beaten whites of two eggs. Orange ice is made in the same way, using oranges instead of lemons.

6 : *Raspberry ice*

350 ml raspberry juice, 700 ml clarified sugar, 525 ml water, juice of one lemon. Currant ice is made in the same way.
17 degrees.

7 : *Strawberry ice*

350 ml strawberry juice, 350 ml heavy cream, 700 ml clarified sugar, 175 ml water, juice of one lemon, and some red food coloring.

8 : *Sour cherry ice*

Crush 250 g sour cherries with pits, mix with 525 ml water, and pass through a sieve. Then add 700 ml clarified sugar. Before freezing, add 3 beaten egg whites. 17 degrees.

9 : *Pineapple ice*

87 ml pineapple juice or 125 g crushed pineapple are blended with 700 ml clarified sugar, 175 ml water, juice of 2 lemons, and 1 beaten egg white. 17 degrees.

10 : *Tutti frutti ice*

To frozen lemon ice add diced stewed fruit. Serve in glasses.

11 : *Punch à la glace*

To 700 ml vanilla ice add 3 jiggers rum or some arrack. Mix thoroughly and serve in glasses.

12 : *May wine*

Steep woodruff leaves, not washed but with stems removed, in white wine. Mix this with 2 bottles Moselle wine, one bottle champagne, 2 spoons cognac, and carbonated water. Add lemon-flavored sugar, orange slices, and strawberries.

13 : *Gugelhupf à la Rothschild*

720 g flour, 320 g creamed butter, 80 g sugar, 6 yolks, 4 eggs, 50 g yeast, salt, raisins, vanilla sugar, 100 ml milk. Make a sponge with the yeast, 1/4 of the flour, and a little milk. With the rest of the ingredients prepare a dough. Mix the dough little by little with the yeast sponge and let it rise. Bake. After the cake has cooked cover it with chocolate glaze.

14 : *Very good gugelhupf*

Clarify 125 g butter, let it set, and then cream until fluffy. Blend with 5 yolks, 250 g flour, 17 g yeast, salt, 1 tbsp sugar, 175 ml milk. Line the form with almonds.

15 : *Chestnut pudding*

50 g butter, 50 g sugar, 50 g roasted, finely ground chestnuts,
3 egg yolks, and 3 beaten egg whites are steamed in a
ring mold. Fill the center of the ring with stewed
sour cherries.

16 : *Poppy seed strudel*

Make a dough using 500 g flour, 4 yolks, 3 eggs, 34 g yeast,
butter, and enough milk to make it fairly soft. Let the dough
rise. Roll it out. Spread over it with 1/2 liter crushed
poppy seeds, raisins, plenty of sugar, and some honey.
Roll the dough into a loaf, let it rise again,
and bake in a roasting pan.

17 : *Sand cakes*

Prepare a dough of 200 g butter, 200 g sugar, 5 yolks, 4 eggs,
200 g flour. Spread this on a baking sheet and bake. Cut squares
and fill with raspberry jam. Sprinkle with sugar.

18 : *Yeast dough raisin cake*

Prepare a good yeast dough with 375 g flour. Let the dough
rise, then spread it on a baking sheet and let it rise again. Cover
the dough with egg whites, beaten but not stiff, a lot of sugar,
raisins, top with a bit of melted butter. Bake.

19 : *Coffee pudding*

Over a flame stir 250 g flour, 350 ml milk, and 350 ml strong
coffee until the mixture separates from the spoon. Place it in a
bowl and add sugar as needed, 20 egg yolks, 15 beaten
egg whites, lemon essence, also 250 g butter. Steam
this mixture in a mold and serve with punch glaze.

20 : *Punch glaze*

Blend two walnut-sized pieces of butter with two cooking
spoons of flour and mix with a generous pint of boiled sugar.
Boil this mixture down and add to it the juice of 2 lemons,

3 spoons of rum, 2 spoons of maraschino, 2 spoons of
vanilla liqueur, and red food color. Pour over the
coffee pudding.

21 : *Basta Flora cake*

Mix a dough from 167 g flour, 167 g butter, 84 g sugar,
a small tablet of chocolate, 3 yolks, cloves, and cinnamon. Make
a cake out of this mixture and cover it with a lattice of dough.
When baked, fill the lattice with currant preserve.

22 : *Little wreaths*

250 g flour, 100 g sugar, 200 g butter, 2 yolks, grated lemon
rind, a bit of cinnamon, and cloves.

23 : *Brioche*

Place 250 g flour on a board. Remove a small amount and make
a sponge with 17 g yeast. Let this rise. Work the rest of the
flour, the yeast sponge, 34 g sugar, salt into a dough. Let the
dough rise. After it has risen, add the 200 g butter in small
pieces and 3 yolks and 1 egg, well whisked. Work the dough
with your hands and let it rise. Bake in a charlotte mold.

24 : *Sand cake*

Beat together 125 g sugar, 4 eggs, 4 yolks. Then add 125 g
cornstarch and 125 g butter.

25 : *Snowballs*

Mix 250 g flour, 100 g butter, 3 yolks, salt, sugar, cinnamon,
grated lemon rind, and 3 spoons of wine and some heavy cream
into a batter. Beat it well and then let it rest. Roll out the dough
and with a cookie cutter, cut out rounds about 2-1/2 inches
across. With a pastry wheel, cut through the rounds four times
without cutting into the border. This will form three strips
attached to the border. Fry in deep fat. Fruit juice or
chaudeau may be served with the snowballs.

26 : *Chaudeau*
125 g sugar, 350 ml wine, 14 yolks.

27 : *Chocolate cream slices*
Prepare a batter of 9 eggs, 200 g sugar, 100 g cornstarch,
100 g cake flour. Spread the batter over the whole baking sheet
and bake. Cut into four strips and fill each pair of strips with the
following cream: Beat 3 yolks, 2 eggs, and 200 g sugar over
boiling water until fairly thick. Let the mixture cool. In the
meantime, cream 200 g butter with 200 g chocolate
and slowly blend in the egg cream.
Decorate the tops of the cakes.

28 : *Tea pastries*
Twenty-two eggs and 34 g sugar are beaten until foamy, then
add 700 ml water or milk with 100 g satangali and 3.7 kg flour.
Prepare the dough one day in advance. Then form bars,
2 inches long and one finger wide. The bars can be
sprinkled with fennel. Bake until nicely yellow.

29 : *Vanilla crescents*
Cream thoroughly 120 g butter, blend in 60 g blanched ground
almonds, 60 g sugar, 100 g flour. Form crescents, bake them
to a pale yellow, and roll them in vanilla sugar.

30 : *Sticks à la Pálffy*
Quickly work together into a dough 134 g flour, 67 g butter,
34 g sugar, salt, and 3 tbsp milk. Let the dough rest for a bit.
Form little sticks as thin as knitting needles. Place them
on a lightly buttered baking sheet and brush them
with egg. Bake them in a moderate oven.

31 : *Yeast pretzel*
Make a soft dough of 500 g flour, 3 eggs, 60 g sugar, some salt,
milk, and 40 g yeast. Let the dough rest for 1 hour, then chill it.
When the dough is properly chilled, spread it on a board.

For each 500 g of dough, fold in 120 g butter kneaded until it is elastic and roll three times like puff pastry. During the third rolling add raisins. Form pretzels, let them rise, and bake them in a medium hot oven. Cover the pretzels with lemon icing. (These are genuine Karlsbader pretzels according to the recipe from the baker Mannl of Karlsbad.)

32 : *Cabbage strudel*
Chop fresh cabbage fairly fine, salt it, and let it sit for a while. Then squeeze out the accumulated liquid. Sauté the cabbage in good lard. Pull strudel dough into a sheet, spread the cabbage over it, and roll it up and bake.

33 : *Bombe à la Esterházy*
Chocolate ice cream around a center of whipped cream. Decorate with cornets.

34 : *Strawberry bombe*
Strawberry ice around a center of whipped cream. Decorate with whole strawberries and sponge cake.

35 : *Chestnut bombe à la Russe*
Chestnut ice cream with whipped cream and sliced stewed fruit.

36 : *Apricot bombe*
Apricot ice cream around a center of whipped cream. Decorate with sliced stewed apricots and lady fingers.

37 : *Coffee praline bombe*
Hazelnut ice cream topped with whipped cream and decorated with sugared coffee beans.

38 : *Cold chocolate soufflé*
Stir 6 yolks, 200 g sugar, 500 ml heavy cream over a flame, add 300 g fine warm chocolate. Mix well and pour the cream through a fine sieve. Place on ice to cool. Beat 750 ml heavy

cream until firm and blend with the cooled cream. Pour the mixture into a silver soufflé bowl. Place strips of paper around the border of the bowl so that it can be filled to the top. Place the bowl into ice for 3 hours. Cut off the paper, sprinkle the soufflé with cake crumbs and sugar, and serve.

39 : *Horseshoes*
On a board work into a dough 134 g flour, 67 g butter, and a sponge made with 17 g yeast. Form horseshoes and with a finger press 7 holes into the horseshoes to represent the nail holes. Let the dough rise. Before putting horseshoes in the oven, place a small piece of butter in each hole and sprinkle the horseshoes with salt.

40 : *Swedish punch*
Bring a liter of water to a boil, then add 540 g sugar. Boil this down to 1 liter. Add 1 liter arrack, one spoon at a time, and mix well. Pour the punch into bottles, close them tightly with corks, and store. Serve cold.

41 : *Strawberry punch*
Pass wild strawberries through a sieve and mix with sugar. Add one bottle of Rhine wine, 4 glasses of madeira, 2 glasses arrack. Set in ice. Serve in glasses with small pastries.

42 : *Gingerbread*
Boil 1/4 liter milk with 350 g sugar and 45 g butter. In a bowl, mix well 460 g flour, 2.5 g cinnamon, 7.5 g crushed cloves, 100 g finely chopped candied citron, 100 g almonds. Whisk in the boiling milk and one egg. Fold this batter into a floured cloth and let it rest one or two days. Then halve the dough and blend into each half 7.5 g potash dissolved in a spoonful of rum. Knead the dough well, roll it out fairly thin, and cut out whatever shapes you like. Bake the gingerbread on waxed baking sheets in a moderate oven and cover with lemon icing. Lemon icing:

To a bowl of finely sifted sugar, add two egg whites and
the juice of 1 lemon. Stir for one half hour and leave
overnight in a warm place.

43 : *English biscuits (cookies)*

Cream until fluffy 100 g butter, add 400 g vanilla sugar, 3 eggs,
15 g baking powder, 125 ml heavy cream. Blend well and stir in
800 g flour. Turn the dough out on a board, work it well, and
let it rest for a while. Then roll it out to knife-edge thickness,
cut out rounds about 2-1/2 inches in diameter, and shape
the cookies by pressing them onto a curved grater.
Bake the cakes on a well-buttered baking sheet.

44 : *Chestnut gâteau*

Boil 750 g of nice chestnuts, cut them fine, and puree them.
Cream 7 yolks and 7 tbsp confectioners' sugar and fold in
7 beaten egg whites and the chestnut puree.
Bake in a slow oven.

45 : *Hard Linzer gâteau*

Cream 250 g butter with 167 g sugar. Add 4 sieved hard-boiled
egg yolks, some grated lemon rind, cinnamon, and a mixture of
250 g flour and 125 g grated, blanched almonds. Place part of
the dough in a round cake pan. Cover with currant preserve.
From the rest of the dough form a lattice. Brush the
lattice with egg and bake.

46 : *Cinnamon cookies*

Work together on a board 250 g flour, 250 g butter,
250 g sugar, 250 g unblanched almonds, 2 teaspoons
cinnamon, 1 teaspoon crushed cloves, grated rind of lemon,
1 large or 2 small egg whites. Roll the dough to knife-edge
thickness, cut out cookies, brush them with water,
and sprinkle them with sugar. Bake.

47 : *Orange soufflé à la Monte Carlo*

Cut off the upper thirds of oranges. Squeeze out the juice. Whip one egg white per two oranges, add one spoon sugar, the juice of the oranges, and fill this mixture into the hollowed-out oranges. Place them on a baking sheet, sprinkle them generously with sugar. Bake the oranges for a few minutes in a hot oven. Red oranges are especially nice when served in a suitably folded napkin.

48 : *Stirred sponge cake*

Ten yolks, 267 g sugar, lemon essence, vanilla, 267 g cornstarch, and 12 whipped egg whites.

49 : *Sand cake*

Butter to the weight of 3 eggs, flour to the weight of 6 eggs, 500 g sugar, 9 eggs, lemon flavoring.

50 : *Russian cream*

Stir until foamy 10 yolks, 250 g sugar, lemon juice, plenty of fine rum. Add a quart of whipped cream. Set with gelatine.

51 : *English whip*

The juice of 10 oranges and 5 lemons, 10 yolks, 250 g sugar, 1 tbsp potato starch. Whip these ingredients over a flame. Let the mixture cool and add one quart whipped cream and gelatine.

52 : *Chocolate Pudding*

Cream 267 g butter, blend in 267 g sugar, 267 g chocolate, 16 yolks, 200 g grated almonds, 16 beaten egg whites, and 16 hard rolls with crusts cut off, cubed, and softened in milk. Steam the pudding and pour chocolate cream over it.

53 : *English pie*

Invert a small bowl in an ovenproof dish. Surround the bowl with green gooseberries, until the dish is full. Add 4 tbsp water, 4 tbsp sugar, and some vanilla (various other sliced fruit could also be used). Cover the dish with a butter dough and bake it.

54 : *Cookies à la Sarah Bernhardt*

On a board work together 140 g flour, 140 g butter, 30 g sugar, 1 yolk, 70 g chocolate. Form small balls, set them on a baking sheet, wet your finger and make a depression in each ball and place in it half a blanched almond. Bake in a slow oven.

55 : *Very good cherry cake*

Remove the crust of seven hard rolls, cut them into very small cubes, and soften the cubes in milk. Cream 200 g butter, add 8 yolks one at a time, then 200 g ground blanched almonds, 34 g vanilla sugar, 1 kg black cherries. Finish by lightly folding in the softened cubes and 8 beaten egg whites.

56 : *Chocolate crescents*

On a board work together 140 g grated chocolate, 140 g ground almonds, 2 beaten egg whites, spices, and lemon flavoring. Shape the dough into crescents and bake in a slow oven. Cover the crescents with chocolate glaze.

57 : *Almond cream*

Cream 140 g butter and 140 g vanilla sugar, add 140 g ground almonds, 4 yolks, 4 tbsp very strong coffee, and blend well. Line a charlotte mold with lady fingers moistened with liqueur. Fill the mold with the cream and set it on ice for two hours. Turn out the dessert on a serving plate and decorate it with stewed fruit and whipped cream.

58 : *Crayfish salad*

Prepare with mayonnaise and serve with parsley, vinegar, and oil, with mustard on the side.

59 : *Pistachio cream*

Figure on 200–300 g pistachio nuts per person. Crush the pistachio nuts in a marble mortar, add a few finely ground blanched almonds, and pour a little spun sugar over the mixture. Mix well and press through a cloth. Then add whipped cream and clarified gelatine.
Let the cream set on ice.

60 : *Peppermint punch*

Put peppermint leaves into a jug, add one bottle carbonated water, juice of 1/2 orange, juice of 1 lemon, chopped lemon rind, 3 liqueur glasses cognac, 3 liqueur glasses curaçao, some ice. Let stand in ice for two hours and before serving add a bottle of Moët et Chandon.

61 : *Peach punch*

Sliced peaches, sugar, lemons, oranges, white wine, champagne, and carbonated water. Cool on ice.

62 : *Sponge cake puffs*

Whip until fluffy 250 g sugar, 15 egg yolks, vanilla flavoring. Blend in 9 beaten egg whites mixed with 250 g flour. Drop the batter from a teaspoon onto a buttered baking sheet and bake to a pale color. Fill cakes with apricot jam and sprinkle them with sugar.

63 : *Genuine Baden coffee candies*

500 ml strong coffee, 500 ml spun sugar, 500 ml whipped cream, vanilla. Prepare 500 ml coffee using 80 g ground beans. Add the spun sugar, the whipped cream, and a bit of vanilla. Place the mixture in a cooking pot that is fairly large in proportion to the mixture. Cook the mixture, while stirring constantly, until it is thick. This will take from 3/4 to 1 hour. Turn out the mixture on a marble board that has been coated with fine almond oil. When the mixture has cooled, cut it with a pastry wheel into

candy-sized pieces. With a knife, loosen the pieces from the
board. Wipe off the oil and wrap the candy in fine paper.

64 : *Salt sticks*

Make a sponge using 134 g flour, 84 g butter, 1/2 liter yeast in
milk. Moisten the dough with lukewarm milk. Form thin sticks,
brush them with egg, sprinkle them with caraway seeds and
coarse salt. Let the sticks rise and bake them.

65 : *Gervais cheese*

Pour sweet or sour cream into a thin cloth. Tie the cloth into a
bundle; hang it up to let the liquid drip out. When the dripping
has stopped, the cheese is ready to serve.

66 : *Bohemian dumpling*

Thoroughly beat a dumpling batter. Cut the crusts off hard
rolls, cube, and sauté them in butter. Mix the croutons with the
batter; add salt. Tie the mixture into a napkin and cook in
boiling water for 1/2 hour. The dumpling should be
the size of an ox's head.

67 : *Peaches*

Blanch nice peaches, peel them, and arrange them on a serving
plate, sprinkle them with macaroon crumbs and sugar.
Pour maraschino and kirsch over the peaches and
set them alight before serving.

68 : *Peaches and raspberries*

Peel blanched peaches and set aside to cool. Shell fresh walnuts
and sprinkle nut halves over the peaches. Then pour a
generously sugared raspberry puree over the peaches.

69 : *Fruit in cognac*

Cut into thin slices several nice pieces of fruit and place
them into a glass bowl. Pour cognac over the fruit, cover, and
set on ice. Instead of cognac, kirsch, maraschino, or
champagne may be used.

70 : *Coffee liqueur*

Soak 3 g vanilla beans cut into pieces in 1/2 liter alcohol and let this stand in a warm place for several days. Boil 1 kg sugar with 1/2 liter water until the sugar forms threads. In the meantime make 1/2 liter black coffee using 250 g freshly roasted beans. Cook the coffee with the sugar to keep the sugar from hardening. When the mixture is cold blend it with the strained alcohol and pour it into a large bottle. Keep the bottle for several weeks at room temperature. Then decant the liqueur into smaller bottles. The older the liqueur, the better it will be.

71 : *Napoleon bars*

Stir together 134 g sugar, 3 eggs, 2 yolks, add 67 g flour. Roast 134 g finely slivered almonds in sugar and add to the batter. Spread the batter on a baking sheet and bake only lightly. Cut the cake into serving-size slices and fill with apricot jam.

72 : *Hazelnut bread*

Stir well 134 g sugar and 8 yolks. Add 134 g ground hazelnuts, 100 g grated chocolate, 4 beaten egg whites, 50 g bread crumbs. Bake either in a loaf pan or form a loaf and bake it on a cookie sheet.

73 : *Chocolate bread*

Blend 267 g sugar with 8 yolks, add 8 beaten egg whites, 267 g grated chocolate, 67 g ground almonds, 134 g flour. Bake in a loaf pan.

74 : *Granita of strawberries with small pastries*

Pass strawberries through a sieve, add white wine, a little water, the juice of a few lemons, and sugar. Pass through a fine sieve again and freeze partially. Leave on ice. Blend in whipped cream and vanilla sugar. Cover the ice cream well and bury in ice. Fill champagne glasses with the ice cream, garnish with a few strawberries, and serve with small cakes.

75 : *Sand gâteau*

Beat 16 whole eggs with 500 g sugar over boiling water until thick. Then continue beating until the cream is cold. Blend in 500 g melted butter and 500 g potato starch. Bake in a slow oven and glaze with lemon icing.

76 : *Diplomat pudding*

In a casserole stir 16 yolks, 375 g vanilla sugar, and 1-1/2 liters milk over a flame. Add gelatine and kirsch. First line the mold with cubes of cake, then add the cream. Put on ice.

77 : *Apple rice with meringue*

Cook rice in milk with a piece of vanilla bean. Blend a piece of butter and some sugar into the cooked rice. In the bottom of a buttered fireproof dish spread a layer of rice, then jam, then stewed apples. Sprinkle with a few almonds. Add layers of rice and apples and top with rice and jam. Cover this with a meringue and bake it in a cool oven. Before serving, dust with sugar and decorate with jam.

79 : *Dark Linzer gâteau*

On a pastry board, work 375 g flour, 375 g butter, 250 g sugar, 250 g grated almonds, 3 yolks, cinnamon, and grated lemon rind into a dough. Line a round cake pan with part of the dough. Spread the dough with jam and cover with a lattice made with the rest of the dough. Brush with egg and bake.

80 : *Sicilian cake*

Prepare dough for a Linzer gâteau. Place part of it into a cake pan. Cover it with the following cream: 1/2 liter milk, 100 g sugar, 67 g flour, 4 yolks, 1 egg, vanilla and cinnamon, a bit of rum. Cover it with a lattice of dough and bake in a slow oven. Serve warm.

81 : *Baked ice cream*

Prepare vanilla ice cream and add orange juice to it. On a fireproof platter spread a meringue mixture and bake it. Let it cool and put the vanilla ice cream on it. Cover this with meringue batter and dust with sugar. Sear it with a red-hot metal scoop. Serve with wafers.

82 : *Hazelnut or almond ice cream*

Prepare a cream without vanilla. For 1 liter cream use 375 g ground almonds or hazelnuts. Pass the nuts with some milk through a sieve, add them to the cream, and freeze. The hazelnuts or almonds must first be roasted in the oven until yellow through and through.

83 : *Ice or pudding à la Nesselrode*

Partly freeze a vanilla cream mixed with some chestnut puree. Add sliced fruit, pistachio, raisins, grapes, well moistened with maraschino, and whipped cream. Pour into a mold and freeze for 3 hours. When serving as a pudding, present with a vanilla cream sauce and whipped cream in a sauceboat.

84 : *Croquembouche*

Prepare a chestnut puree. Boil sugar with a vanilla bean and water until it reaches the brittle stage. Mix the puree and the sugar and make small balls several days before they are needed so that they have time to form a crust. Dip the balls into a brittle sugar syrup, pick them up with a fine skewer, and line the walls of a charlotte mold with them. Turn out the shell formed by the balls and fill it with whipped cream.

85 : *Swallows' nests*

Bake meringue rings. Place one ring on top of the other and set them on a serving platter. Pass chestnut puree through a sieve held over the rings in such a way that strands of puree fall on the rings and hang over the sides. Fill the centers with whipped cream.

86 : *Genuine Pischinger gâteau*

Put in a large bowl 120 g sugar, 2 handfuls peeled, ground
hazelnuts, some vanilla, and 6 eggs. Stir over boiling water until
thick, then let the cream cool. Cream 250 g butter, 80 g sugar,
8 squares softened chocolate and add the egg cream one tbsp at
a time. Spread this filling between Karlsbad wafers, making
seven layers, and cover the cake with a chocolate glaze.

87 : *Walnut gâteau*

Stir 200 g sugar, 12 yolks, 2 eggs, until fluffy, then add
cinnamon, cloves, and grated lemon rind. Fold in 234 g ground
walnuts and 67 g bread crumbs with 12 beaten egg whites. Bake
in two layers and put them together with jam. Cover the cake
with cream-colored icing and decorate with walnut halves.

88 : *Chocolate gâteau*

Cream 134 g butter, 134 g sugar, 134 g softened chocolate
until fluffy, add one at a time 8 yolks, 134 g ground almonds,
50 g bread crumbs, and 8 beaten egg whites. Bake, let the cake
cool, spread it with apricot jam and chocolate icing.

89 : *Vanilla Bavarian cream*

In a heavy cooking pot combine 8 yolks, 200 g sugar,
1/2 liter milk, vanilla. Beat this mixture over the heat until
it forms a cream. Add gelatine and put the cream on ice. When
it is cold, fold in 5 beaten egg whites. Color part of the cream
red and pour it into a mold, add the rest of the cream. Place
the mold on ice. Turn it out on a serving dish and
serve with cookies.

90 : *Fruit ice in wine*

Use any kind of fruit ice, but the best are strawberry, raspberry,
and currant ices. Add some sugar to the ice and equal quantities
of Moët et Chandon champagne and Johannisberger wine plus
one tbsp arrack. Freeze the mixture. The resulting ice should
be grainy and not too solid. Serve in glasses with straws.

Créme, Gelée és Bavaroisnak.

309   300   303

312   316   313

Bordure-formák Geléenek.

318—327   322—329

Savarin-forma.   Savarin-forma.

325   320   Gelée-forma a.

A few of the many molds for puddings and pastry offered in an 1893 cook-book with a shopping catalog in the appendix. Ornate forms of these kinds would have been considered normal kitchen equipment. From József Hegyesi, *A Legujabb Házi Czukraszat Kézikönyve* (Budapest, 1893).

91 : *Fürst Pückler cream*

Whip heavy cream and divide it into 3 parts. Color one-third
red and add strawberry puree to it; color the second part brown
with chocolate; add vanilla to the third. Sugar all three parts
generously. Fill a mold first with the brown cream,
then the vanilla cream, and top with the red cream.
Bury in ice and freeze.

92 : *Nut roll*

Blend 167 g sugar and 8 yolks in a mixing bowl until fluffy.
Add grated lemon rind, 8 beaten egg whites, and 100 g sifted
flour. Bake on a cookie sheet. Then beat 100 g sugar, 5 yolks,
and 1 whole egg until fluffy. Add 5 beaten egg whites, 84 g
ground almonds, 67 g bread crumbs, and grated lemon rinds.
Mix thoroughly and bake on a cookie sheet. For the filling, beat
5 egg whites, add 67 g sugar and 67 g finely chopped nuts.
Spread the filling evenly over the sheet that was baked
first, cover it with the second sheet. Roll up the
cake and cover it with white icing.

93 : *Hazelnut pudding*

Cream thoroughly 375 g butter, 375 g sugar, add 32 egg yolks
and 32 trimmed rolls softened in milk. Add 32 beaten
egg whites and 267 g ground hazelnuts. Bake.

94 : *Gâteau with foam topping*

On a board work a dough made of 134 g flour,
134 g butter, 134 g sugar, 134 g ground almonds, and 1 yolk.
Bake the dough in a round cake pan. Prepare the following
topping: Beat 8 egg whites. Melt 3 tbsp apricot jam, or any
other jam, add 250 g of sugar spun in 350 ml water, and
8 sheets of gelatin. Blend the sugar mixture with the
beaten egg whites and spread on the cake in the pan.
Put on ice.

95 : *Chocolate roll*

Stir well 67 g softened chocolate with 5 yolks and 100 g sugar.
Mix with 100 g ground almonds, 4 beaten egg whites. Spread
mixture on a cookie sheet and bake. Spread with jam and roll.
Cover with icing.

96 : *Fruit cake*

Cut 100 g butter into 134 g flour, add 50 g sugar, 1-1/2 egg
yolks, 1 spoon vinegar, and some salt. Work this into a dough.
Spread a thin layer of the dough on a baking sheet and form a
border all around. Cover the dough generously with bread
crumbs, apple slices and top it with currants. Sprinkle with
plenty of sugar and bake. This cake can be made with
any kind of fruit.

97 : *Stephanie slices*

320 g flour, 240 g butter, 100 g sugar, 3 yolks, juice of
1/2 lemon, and grated lemon rind are worked into a dough.
Divide the dough in half, bake each half on a cookie sheet.
Spread cranberry preserve between the two layers,
brush the top with egg, sprinkle with
crystal sugar, and bake.

98 : *Hohensalzburg cake*

Sugar to the weight of 6 eggs, flour to the weight of
4 eggs, 6 eggs. The eggs and sugar are stirred for 1/2 hour,
then the flour is blended in. The batter is baked in a well-
greased and floured tall mold. Cut the top off the finished cake,
make a hollow in the cake, and fill it with whipped cream or a
custard. Replace the lid and glaze the cake with chocolate icing.
Icing: 134 g sugar, 134 g chocolate. Boil the sugar until it
forms threads, melt the chocolate, and add sugar to the
chocolate, a little at a time. Do not let it boil. If the icing
becomes too thick, thin it with boiling water.

A cake worthy of its name was required to be ornamented as well as delicious. From József Hegyesi, *A Legujabb Házi Czukraszat Kézikönyve*
(Budapest, 1893).

99 : *American truffles*
Cream puffs are rolled in grated chocolate and sugar.

100 : *Almond sticks*
Cream 120 g butter, add 140 g sugar, 140 g ground, blanched
almonds, 3 yolks, 1 egg, 140 g flour. Spread the batter on a
baking sheet and bake. Cut into bars or form small tarts
decorated with jam.

101 : *Sponge cake with meringue*
Bake a very thin layer of sponge cake on a sheet. Cut cake into
slices. Using a pastry tube, pipe designs onto the slices with a
meringue made of one beaten egg white to 50 g of sugar.

102 : *Cakes à la Brabant*
1. 200 g flour, 140 g butter, a very little bit of sugar, 1 yolk,
lemon juice and grated rind, a trace of salt.
2. 90 g flour, 70 g butter, 35 g ground almonds, 1/2 yolk.
Between these two layers, spread a small amount of raw
or cooked fruit. Cut slices and bake. Pour lemon icing
over the slices and remove from baking sheet.

103 : *Piquant fruit (French)*
For 8–10 persons take 8–10 pineapple slices. Cut the slices
very fine and place them in a shallow bowl. Then add a layer of
finely sliced oranges. Whip a pint of heavy cream, add vanilla,
sugar, 6–8 teaspoons kirsch, 6–8 teaspoons maraschino.
Pour this mixture over the fruit, decorate with strawberries
and grapes. Put the dish on ice and serve it cold.

104 : *Macaroon gâteau*
Beat until foamy 200 g ground almonds, 400 g sugar,
10 egg whites. Then add 60 g flour, some vanilla, and lemon
flavoring. Bake two sheets and fill them with a good filling.
Decorate with macaroons.

105 : *Noodles à la Ödenburg*

Prepare a good noodle pudding. Place half of it in an ovenproof dish and bake lightly. Over this spread poppy seeds roasted in butter, some sugar, cinnamon, and lemon flavoring blended with a cup of milk. Top with the other half of the noodle pudding and bake in a slow oven.

106 : *Fine pastry rum pretzels*

210 g flour, 14 small or 12 large yolks, 70 g sugar, 70 g butter, vanilla, and a tablespoon of fine rum are worked into a dough on a board. Roll the dough until it separates from the rolling pin. Form pretzels or other shapes. Place them on a buttered baking sheet and bake them in a fairly hot oven.

107 : *Semolina strudel*

Beat 500 g butter and 167 g vegetable shortening or lard until fluffy, blend in 24 yolks, one at a time. Mix in thoroughly 6 cups semolina and 6 cups heavy cream, add salt. Fold in beaten egg whites. Prepare a strudel dough, fill it with the semolina mixture, and roll it into medium-sized loaves. With the floured handle of a cooking spoon, mark off four to six portions of dough, then cut through them with a knife. Press the cut edges together to form closed pockets and cook in boiling water. Pour melted butter over the strudels and serve them with prune butter or stewed cherries.

108 : *A very good brown cherry cake*

Stir 200 g sugar and 12 egg yolks until fluffy. Add 234 g ground almonds, some cinnamon and allspice, fold in 9 beaten egg whites, 50 g dark bread crumbs moistened with red wine, 1-1/2 squares chocolate. Cover with cherries and bake partially, then add more cherries and finish baking.

109 : *Cream puffs or choux à la crème*

Boil 1 liter water and 400 g butter, add 500 g fine flour, 34 g sugar. Stir over a flame until the mixture detaches itself from the pan. Then mix in well 15 eggs. With a tablespoon

drop small balls of the dough onto a buttered baking sheet.
Sprinkle slivered almonds over them and bake. When cooled,
fill the pastry with a fairly thick vanilla cream.

110 : *Bishop's bread*
Stir 200 g sugar and 12 yolks until fluffy, add 200 g flour,
12 beaten egg whites, a handful of raisins, some slivered
almonds, and candied lemon rind. Bake and
cut thin slices. Toast the slices.

111 : *Tutti-frutti ice à la napolitaine*
Rub through a sieve melon puree, vanilla essence, and
orange juice. Partly freeze the liquid, then mix with whipped
cream and cubed pineapple. Finish freezing in a bombe mold.
To serve, decorate with candied orange slices.

112 : *Gingerbread rounds (Pfeffernüsse)*
Stir for half an hour 250 g sugar with 3 large eggs, then
add 8 g cinnamon, 5 g cloves, some nutmeg, grated rind of one
lemon, 15 g finely diced candied citron, a bit of pepper, and
250 g flour. Work the dough vigorously, roll it, and cut out
small rounds with a cookie cutter. Place them on a cookie sheet
and let them stand in the kitchen for 24 hours. Then turn
them over so that the damp side is on top. Bake them
to a light yellow.

113 : *Mocha cream bars*
Beat over heat 250 g sugar with 6 eggs until lukewarm and
fairly thick. Remove the mixture from the heat and continue
beating until it is cold. Lightly blend in 250 g cornstarch.
Spread the batter on a well-greased baking sheet and bake it in
a cool oven. Cut slices. For the filling, beat over a flame until
thick 250 g sugar, 7 yolks, 1 cup very strong coffee. Continue
beating until the mixture is cold. Beat until fluffy 250 g butter
and add to it the cream, a little bit at a time. Fill the cake slices
with this cream and cover the tops with cream as well.
Place the finished cakes on ice until ready to serve.

114 : *Fine sugar dough for fruit gâteau*
An exact weight of 500 g flour, 500 g butter, 250 g sugar,
and 4 egg yolks.

115 : *Sugar dough for small tarts or strawberry cake*
300 g flour, 250 g butter, 100 g sugar, 4 hard-cooked yolks
passed through a sieve.

116 : *Cheese cake*
Pass cream cheese through a sieve, add sugar, butter,
and eggs depending on the size cake you want, and stir this
well. Mix a short dough of 500 g flour, 250 g butter, 4 yolks, a
handful of blanched almonds, ground, 134 g sugar, and grated
lemon rind. Roll the dough to cover the whole baking sheet,
but not too thin. Bake until only half done. Spread the filling
over the cake, sprinkle with brown and white raisins,
candied lemon peel, and slivered almonds.
Bake in a slow oven.

117 : *Coffee pudding*
Cream 250 g butter, 250 g sugar, and 16 yolks. Trim 6 rolls,
soak them in strong black coffee. Pass the rolls through a sieve
and add them to the butter mixture. Fold in 12 beaten egg
whites and 250 g blanched, finely chopped almonds. Steam
in a mold. Serve with whipped cream or a coffee cream.

118 : *Nut bars with whipped cream*
Stir 250 g sugar and 14 yolks until foamy. Fold in
12 egg whites beaten until stiff, 250 g finely chopped hazelnuts,
67 g cornstarch. Bake on a baking sheet in a cool oven.
Slice the cake and fill with whipped cream.

119 : *Nut crescents*
Make a sponge using 500 g flour and 50 g compressed
yeast. Add 34 g sugar, 3 eggs, grated rind of 1/2 lemon, salt,
67 g melted butter. Beat the ingredients into a soft dough with

some lukewarm milk. Spread the dough on a board, place 134 g
cold, washed butter in the center, and fold the dough over
crosswise. Roll the dough four times at 10-minute intervals.
For the filling, blend well 84 g finely chopped walnuts, 167 g
sugar, vanilla from one vanilla bean, and some milk. Roll the
dough, spread it with melted butter, and cut it into 32 triangles.
Cover the triangles evenly with the filling and roll them into
croissants. Let them rise on a baking sheet and bake them
in a hot oven. If desired, the croissants may be covered
with a thin vanilla glaze.

120 : *Paris gâteau*
In a bowl mix well 280 g confectioners' sugar, 280 g finely
chopped almonds, 70 g candied citron, 150 g candied orange
peel, 30 g pistachio — all finely slivered; add vanilla. Fold in
10 beaten egg whites. Bake in a well-buttered round cake pan
at low heat. This cake must rest for a few days
before it is good to eat.

121 : *Russian punch gâteau*
Beat until fluffy 234 g sugar and 14 yolks. Blend in lightly
200 g flour and 12 beaten egg whites. Place 1/3 of this batter
into a round cake pan. Color the second third red and put it
into a second pan. Put the last third into a pan and bake all
three at moderate heat. After the layers have cooled, cut the red
one into cubes. Boil sugar until thickened, add rum and lemon
juice to make about 350 ml, and soak the cake cubes in the
liquid. Slice the first ring into two layers and fill with jam,
place the softened cubes over it, top with the third ring,
and cover with red rum icing.

122 : *Linzer gâteau*
Cream until fluffy 250 g butter, 200 g sugar, grated lemon rind.
Stir in 5 yolks and 1 egg, lightly blend in 300 g cake flour.
Bake in a slow oven.

123 : *White almond cake*

Stir 200 g sugar and 12 yolks until fluffy. Add finely diced candied citron and grated lemon peel. Fold in lightly 12 egg whites beaten until very stiff, 250 g finely chopped blanched almonds, and 100 g bread crumbs. Bake for 3/4 hour in a cool oven. Spread the cake with jam and cover it with a white icing. Decorate it with candied lemon peel, pistachio, or almonds.

124 : *Chocolate slices with whipped cream*

Stir 250 g sugar and 16 yolks until fluffy. Fold in 16 egg whites beaten until stiff, 267 g ground almonds, 4 squares grated chocolate, and 84 g bread crumbs. For slices, spread the batter about 3/4 inches thick on a baking sheet. The above recipe can also be used for a Stephanie cream gâteau. In that case, bake 6 round layers. Spread whipped cream or an almond cream between the layers. Cover the cake with white icing. Decorate it with red meringue kisses.

125 : *Sacher torte 1*

Beat until very light 134 g butter, 134 g softened chocolate, 134 g sugar. Add 7 yolks, one at a time. Fold in lightly 7 egg whites, beaten until very stiff, and 134 g cornstarch. Bake slowly in a moderate oven. Spread the torte with apricot jam and cover it with chocolate icing.

126 : *Sacher torte 2*

Beat until fluffy 134 g butter, 3 squares softened chocolate, 134 g sugar. Stir in 8 yolks, one at a time. Fold in 8 egg whites beaten until stiff, 134 g ground almonds, and 50 g bread crumbs. Bake slowly at moderate heat. Cover the cake with apricot jam and chocolate icing. A chocolate pudding can be made from the same batter.

127 : *Sour cherry bars*

Cream 250 g rendered beef fat and 250 g sugar until light and fluffy. Add grated lemon rind, 3 eggs, 9 yolks, 250 g flour.

Spread the dough, about two fingers thick, on a greased baking
sheet, cover with 1 kg sour cherries arranged in rows.
Bake in a medium oven.

128 : *Fine almond or spice pudding*
Beat together 500 g butter, 250 g sugar, 24 yolks,
add 500 g almonds chopped fine, 8 g combined of cinnamon
and cloves. Fold in 12 beaten egg whites and 134 g bread
crumbs. Steam the pudding and cover with rum icing.

129 : *Rum icing*
Boil 350 ml water with 500 g sugar until thick. Remove the
sugar from the flame and add 125 ml rum.

130 : *Hard hazelnut gâteau*
7 egg whites, 250 g sugar, 250 g hazelnuts; half of the
sugar beaten in.

131 : *Gâteau à la Trieste*
200 g ground blanched almonds, 200 g sugar, 2 eggs,
10 yolks are stirred together. Add 10 beaten egg whites, 134 g
cake crumbs, slivered nuts. Bake in one layer, assemble
the cake, and frost with lemon icing.

132 : *Rum gâteau*
250 g butter, 250 g sugar, 3 eggs, 4 yolks, 3 tbsp rum,
200 g cornstarch. Bake two layers in round cake pans.
Cover with rum glaze.

133 : *Vanilla cream cakes*
Boil 1 liter water and 400 g butter, add 500 g flour and
34 g sugar. Stir this over a flame. Add 15 eggs. Drop the batter
from a tablespoon onto a baking sheet. Sprinkle chopped,
blanched almonds over the cakes.

134 : *Plum pudding*

Chop 250 g marrow, add 250 g flour, 250 g white raisins,
250 g currants, 250 g bread crumbs, 100 g candied citron,
slivered almonds, 1 egg, and rum. Butter a cloth liberally,
tie up the batter, and cook it for 4 hours. Serve with
rum hard sauce or chaudeau.

135 : *Cabinet slices*

Moisten leftover Rehrücken cake, together with the colored
cookies it was decorated with, with leftover fruit juice. Puree the
mixture through a sieve. Fold in 6 beaten egg yolks and then
6 stiffly beaten egg whites. Spread on a
greased baking sheet and bake.

136 : *Bread pudding*

334 g butter, 334 g sugar, 20 egg yolks, 20 beaten egg whites,
200 g ground almonds, 134 g bread crumbs. Steam the
pudding and pour chaudeau over it.

137 : *Chestnut cream gâteau*

Boil 250 g sugar with 1/2 cup water to the thread stage.
Pour the sugar over 125 g chestnuts that have been passed
through a sieve and stir well. Add slowly 250 g butter. Cover
the cake with a cream and sprinkle with coarse sugar.

138 : *Velvet cake*

Cream until very light 250 g butter and 250 g sugar. Blend in
1 egg, 2 yolks, 250 g cornstarch. Bake and spread
apricot glaze over the cake.

139 : *Coffee cream gâteau*

Into 8 egg whites, beaten until stiff, fold 280 g roasted,
finely ground hazelnuts or almonds, 280 g confectioners' sugar
with vanilla flavoring. Divide the batter in half and bake
in two round cake pans.

For the filling: Stir 150 g vanilla sugar with 4 yolks and
3 tbsp very strong coffee over a flame until the mixture comes
to a boil. Let the mixture cool. Cream 120 g butter and
blend with the cooled egg mixture.
Fill the cake and cover it with coffee icing. For the icing:
Of a total of 260 g confectioners' sugar, mix 2 tbsp with 4 tbsp
strong black coffee. Let the mixture boil up once and slowly add
the remaining sugar, stirring constantly. After about 10 minutes,
pour the rather thick, still-warm icing evenly over the cake.

140 : *Orange marmalade*
Cut 6 oranges and 1 lemon with their rinds into fine strips
and soak these 24 hours in 1/2 liter to 2 liters water. Then boil
the fruit, in the water it was soaked in, for 2 hours. Add 2.25 kg
sugar, boil for another 2 hours. If you want a more liquid
marmalade, use more water. The above quantities are
enough for 1/2 liter to 2 liters of marmalade.

141 : *Meringue*
Beat 6 fresh egg whites and 300 g sugar very stiff. Add vanilla
and lemon juice and stir for about 1 hour. Drop the mass from a
spoon onto wafers. With a piece of stiff white cardboard shape
the desired meringue kisses, stars, rings, etc. Sprinkle the
meringue with finely chopped almonds or sugar. At a low
oven temperature, dry rather than baking the meringues.
The batter can also be colored red or yellow.

142 : *Grape cake*
Cream butter equal to the weight of 4 eggs until fluffy,
add the same weight of sugar, then 4 yolks and last, 4 eggs'
weight of flour and 4 beaten egg whites. Bake the batter in a
shallow pan until half done. Beat 5 egg whites until stiff, mix
with sugar and a handful of slivered almonds. Smooth this
over the dough, cover it with grapes, and finish baking.
Cut the cake into about 1-inch wide slices.

143 : *Napoleon gâteau*

Beat until fluffy 250 g butter and 250 g sugar. Add 12 yolks, 12 egg whites beaten until stiff, mix in 200 g grated almonds and 67 g grated bread crumbs. Bake the batter in two round cake pans. For the filling, beat 8 egg whites until stiff, boil 250 g sugar with a pint of water to the thread stage, and mix with the egg whites.

144 : *Cherries à la Mannheim*

Make a batter from 500 g butter, sweetened to taste, 24 rolls softened in milk and passed through a sieve, 30 yolks, 30 beaten egg whites, 250 g ground, blanched almonds, 1/2 liter heavy cream. Pour half of the batter into a baking pan, cover this with wafers, then cherries, then with the rest of the dough.

145 : *Chocolate pudding*

500 g butter, enough sugar to sweeten, 16 softened rolls passed through a sieve. Stir in 30 yolks, 30 beaten egg whites, 250 g grated almonds, 8 squares chocolate.

146 : *Anise seed bread*

Beat with a whisk until thick 125 g sugar, 4 eggs, 2 yolks. Stir in 200 g flour and some anise seed. Bake in a moderate oven. Store in a cool place.

147 : *Whipped cream sauce*

To a pint of cream add one cooking spoon flour, 4 yolks, and vanilla.

148 : *Hard currant gâteau*

On a board work into a dough 500 g flour, 400 g butter, 134 g sugar, 134 g ground almonds, 4 yolks. Bake three round layers, assemble them with currant jam, and decorate the cake with meringue.

149 : *Gâteau à la Esterházy*
Stir 267 g sugar, 12 yolks, 4 eggs. Add 267 g ground
almonds and 12 beaten egg whites. Bake four round layers.
Spread whipped cream between the layers and cover the
cake with white icing.

150 : *Bread and butter*
Make a dough of 80 g butter, 100 g flour, 70 g grated
almonds, 70 g sugar, 1-1/2 squares chocolate, grated lemon
rind, 1-1/2 yolks. Slice the loaf and spread the slices
with a mixture of 70 g sugar, butter, 3 yolks, and
30 g vanilla sugar.

151 : *Chocolate cake slices*
Cream 200 g butter until fluffy, beat in 200 g sugar and
9 egg yolks. Blend in well 200 g finely chopped almonds and
5 bars grated chocolate. Fold in 9 beaten egg whites. Spread
batter 1/2 inch thick on a baking sheet and bake in a
slow oven. Cut lengthwise strips and fill with
whipped cream. Top with whipped cream.

152 : *Egg punch (for one person)*
Stir until foamy 2 yolks, 6 tsp powdered sugar. Add a
little less than 1/2 cup heavy cream, 1/4 liqueur glass of rum,
and half a liqueur glass of vanilla liqueur. Whisk until the
liquid rises in the glass.

153 : *Caraway seed liqueur*
Set aside for 5–6 days 2–3 tsp caraway seed in 250 ml alcohol
and 1 cup water. As for the rest, treat like vanilla liqueur
but do not tint.

154 : *Orange liqueur*
1/2 liter 40 percent alcohol, 1/2 liter water, 500 g sugar, and
1/2 liter water.

155 : *Hazelnut stars*
Beat until stiff 8 egg whites, stir them for half an hour with
500 g sugar. Set aside one cup of this mixture. To the
remaining mixture, add 4 g of crushed vanilla bean, 125 g finely
ground hazelnuts, 125 g finely chopped almonds; blend well.
Spread the batter on a board sprinkled with sugar and roll it
out. Cut out stars or other shapes. Place the cookies on a baking
sheet spread with wax. Glaze them with the remaining cup
of egg white mixture and bake at a low temperature.

156 : *Tea cakes*
Stir 2 eggs with 125 g sugar, mix with 125 g flour. With a
pastry bag and tube squeeze the dough into various shapes. Let
the cakes stand to dry for several hours, then bake them in a
cool oven. Decorate the cakes with dyed crystal sugar.
The cakes will look very pretty.

157 : *Gingerbread à l'Elise (Nürnberg gingerbread)*
Stir for half an hour 6 eggs with 500 g sugar, add 17 g
cinnamon, grated nutmeg, finely chopped rind of 2 lemons,
84 g candied orange peel and 84 g candied citron, 500 g
ground almonds, not blanched. Mix the ingredients well, spread
the batter on round wafers, and bake. After the cakes have
cooled, cover them with white icing or chocolate glaze,
sprinkle with sugar, and let them dry on top of the stove.

158 : *White gingerbread*
Beat 10 eggs with 560 g sugar until fluffy and thick.
Blend in 560 g flour, 420 g finely chopped blanched almonds,
rind of 1 lemon, 17 g cloves, 17 g cinnamon, 2 knife tips of
potash, 17 g cardamon, some finely chopped candied citron,
140 g candied orange peel. Cut wafers into oblong shapes,
cover them with the dough. Place the gingerbreads on a baking
sheet covered with paper, sprinkle them with sugar, and place
1/2 almond in one corner of each gingerbread.
Bake at moderate heat.

Another version: 500 g sugar, 500 g flour, 12 eggs, 375 g almonds, 125 g candied citron, 125 g candied orange peel, 16.7 g cinnamon, some cloves and cardamon, 2 knife tips potash. Beat the sugar and 12 yolks until fluffy. Fold in the beaten egg whites last. The gingerbread is finished as above. Using only half the listed ingredients yields a large number of gingerbread cookies.

The following recipes were found scribbled on a loose sheet of paper, in a different handwriting, between the pages of the notebook. They are of interest historically because Franz Joseph was very fond of gugelhupf.

Gugelhupf

250 g butter, 400 g flour, 5 egg yolks, 5 whole eggs, 34 g yeast, 1/2 cup milk, sugar, and salt. Cream the butter.

My Gugelhupf

500 g flour, 250 g butter, 4 whole eggs, 4 yolks, milk, salt and sugar, 34 g yeast, raisins, 380 g flour, 210 g butter, 5 eggs, 2 whole, 3 yolks, 20 g yeast.

Rothschild Gugelhupf

720 g flour, 320 g butter, 80 g sugar, 6 yolks, 4 eggs, 30 g yeast, salt, vanilla, raisins, 100 ml milk. Cream the butter, use one-fourth of the flour to form a sponge with the yeast. Add the rest of the ingredients, a bit at a time. Pour the dough into a gugelhupf mold, let it rise, and bake. After the cake has cooled, cover it with chocolate glaze.

Gugelhupf

½ Pf. Butter 24 Loth Mehl
5 Dotter 5 ganze Eier
2 L. Germ ½ Schale Milch
Zucker und Salz
    den Butter abtreiben

Fein Gugelhupf

1 Pf. Mehl ½ Pf. Butter
4 ganze Eier 4 Dotter
Milch Salz und Zucker
2 L. Germ Rosinen

38 dk Mehl
21 " Butter
5 Eier 2 ganze 3 Dotter
2 dk. Germ

NOTES

Gertrud Graubart Champe

The recipes in Katharina Schratt's notebook represent a cuisine that is sufficiently different from modern American cooking to seem remote and occasionally quite strange. And yet an experienced cook could probably obtain good results from most of them after a little tinkering. However, there is a more reliable way to approach the Viennese cuisine of the turn of the century. In the next section of this book, Chef Louis Szathmáry offers a selection of tested, modernized recipes. Working with these recipes and comparing them with the originals is like attending a specialized cooking school. And what is more, following the recipes gives delectable results.

The purpose of the notes, then, is not to make "Cookbook, 1905" into a usable cookbook but to make it possible to read this collection as a document of culinary history. In addition to explaining some unfamiliar cooking terms, the notes concentrate on the names of the recipes, which may prove to be significant. (Note numbers refer to the numbers in the original collection.) It is true that several of the recipes in this collection are for classical French preparations whose names have no relation at all to the time and place we are concerned with here. There are other names that might not be so innocent, however.

In the era with which this book is concerned, there was a custom at formal dinners of sending messages through the names of dishes. For example, when Crown Prince Franz Ferdinand of Austria and his wife visited the king and queen of England, a state dinner on their last evening celebrated the excellent relations between the two countries. At the head of the menu was Consommé Brittania, while the dessert was named Charlotte Viennoise. Since there was a written menu lying at each place at a formal dinner, guests knew the names of the dishes and could think what they wished about them. The names of great families, battlefields, generals, and cultural figures with an Austrian or Hungarian connection are numerous in this collection and help us to picture the setting in which the dishes were served.

1. *Charles-Maurice de Talleyrand-Périgord*, 1754–1838: Celebrated diplomat, churchman, and statesman. Talleyrand believed in the importance of a strong Austria for European stability and therefore worked secretly behind the scenes in favor of Austria rather than of Napoleon, his emperor. He was one of France's greatest gastronomes; the illustrious chef Carême was his cook. Talleyrand considered the magnificence of his table to be an indispensable tool of diplomacy. A similar idea probably had something to do with the style of Katharina Schratt's table as well.

   croustade: A shape made of fried bread or baked pastry crust, used as a base or foundation for serving delicately cooked fish, game, ragouts, or other meat entrées.

   salpicon: A mixture of foods, such as game, fish, poultry, *foie gras*, truffles, and mushrooms, all separately cooked and then bound in a suitable sauce. Sometimes the salpicon is filled into a pastry case. It is interesting to note that in elegant kitchens there were elegant ways to use leftovers. (See also *forcemeat*, note 6.)

   demi-glaze: A sauce reduced until it is almost thick enough for glazing.

4. This recipe can be made with shrimp, lobster, or various kinds of crayfish. The terminology for shellfish is even more confused in English than in German.

6. *forcemeat*: A mixture of ingredients minced or chopped and spiced. Forcemeats are used to stuff or garnish eggs, fish, poultry, game, meat, vegetables, etc. Usually, forcemeats are given substance by the addition of flour or bread moistened with milk or stock. They are then bound with eggs.

   quenelles: Tiny dumplings made of finely pureed meat or fish and bound with egg whites. When cream is added, these may be called mousselines.

7. *patty shell*: A pastry case made of puff pastry.

8. *François Ferdinand Phillipe d'Orléans, Prince de Joinville*, 1818–1900: Third son of King Louis-Phillipe of France, distinguished military figure, popular with the French people for his political views.
julienne: Finely shredded food, sometimes meat but usually vegetables. The julienne and salpicon are made of whatever is available.

9. *caul fat*: Known as *crépine* in French. Membrane in the shape of a net enclosing the lower portion of an animal's intestines, used for wrapping salpicon, sausages, etc. Its function is to protect food from the heat of the oven and to provide fat.

10. *plover*: A wading bird related to the sandpiper. The eggs are considered a great delicacy and may be roasted or lightly boiled. There was a long tradition in Austria that game birds were reserved for the aristocracy and the clergy. In 1885 August Maurer complained in his *Wiener Kochbuch* that only a very few game birds were coming to market because the landowners were either protecting them or eating them themselves.

11. *timbale*: A case, usually made of dough but in this recipe of forcemeat, cooked in a round dish with a fluted edge. When made of dough, the timbale can have either a sweet or a savory filling.
Agnes Sorel, 1422?–1450: Favorite of King Charles VII of France, to whom she bore two daughters.

12. *croquettes*: Cone-shaped forms of ground meat bound with eggs or a sauce, covered with egg and crumbs, and fried in deep fat.

14. *wood grouse*: The largest type of game bird found in Europe, resembling the turkey in size and weight. Modern Austrian cookbooks do not value it highly. Its use is likely to be restricted to hunting banquets. The bird must be young and is

skinned rather than plucked. Generally, only the breast meat, without the fat, is used.

15. *truffle sauce*: Made with brown sauce, red wine, and gelatin. Preparations with Périgord in their names usually have a garnish of truffles, to which *pâté de foie gras* is sometimes added.

16. *bouchées*: Tiny puff pastry patties with savory fillings. The word literally means "mouthful."
madeira sauce: Demi-glaze sauce flavored with madeira.

19. *Jean-Baptiste Colbert, 1619–1683*: Minister of finance for Louis XIV, he successfully practiced mercantilism in his efforts to make France economically independent. Colbert was a great patron of the arts and sciences.

20. *Henri, duc de Rohan, 1579–1638*: French Protestant general, a leader of the Huguenots; or
Louis-René-Edouard, prince de Rohan, 1734–1803: French churchman and politician, cardinal of the Roman Catholic Church. He was French ambassador to Vienna in 1772 but displayed an anti-Austrian attitude which gained him the enmity of the queen, Marie-Antoinette.

24. The asparagus tips in this and other recipes were probably canned, since there was no real asparagus "season" yielding a plentiful supply all at once. Canned food was a new amenity at this time and was very fashionable, because suddenly it was possible to eat foods out of season.

26. *roll*: The crisp Kaiser roll, which is one of the staple breads of Central Europe. Away from large cities in the United States today, the Kaiser roll has a shape similar to the original, but the texture could not be further from the Austrian roll of the same name. A Pepperidge Farm brown-and-serve roll is sometimes the best substitute.

30. *rissole*: Cooked, seasoned ground meat folded into a puff pastry turnover and fried in deep fat.

32. *remoulade sauce*: A piquant mayonnaise-based sauce containing chopped pickles, capers, herbs, and mustard.

33. *roux*: A mixture of flour and butter, cooked slowly, to form the base for a sauce or a thick soup. When the butter and

flour are blended, liquid is added slowly, with constant stirring.

meat glaze: A strong gravy or bone stock reduced by boiling to a brown syrup which sets firm and hard when cold. It can be used alone or to intensify the flavor of another sauce.

34. *ten-penny loaf*: A bread with a good texture, about the size of a one-pound baguette.

35. The chicken was wrapped in bacon because, at that time, the poultry was quite lean.

37. *pâté spices*: Finely ground pepper, bay leaf, cinnamon, nutmeg, ginger, allspice. The liquefied aspic is introduced through two small holes in the top crust.

38. *sauce espagnole*: One of the basic or grand sauces, based on brown stock and a brown roux and cooked for a total of six hours. The sauce is used to make a large number of other sauces.

40. *clarify with egg white*: Broths can be made clear by using egg whites. See, for instance, Chef Louis' recipe for consommé.

41. *St. Hubert*, c. 655–727: Born in the Low Countries. Legend tells us that one day when Hubert was out hunting, he saw a stag bearing a shining cross in its antlers. He decided then to become a Christian. Later, he was made bishop of Tongeren, Liège, and Maastricht. He is the patron saint of hunters.

44. *Gioacchino Antonio Rossini*, 1792–1868: Composer of operas, songs, piano works, and hymn settings. His operatic masterpiece is the *Barber of Seville*. In 1824 he became director of the Théâtre-Italien in Paris.

46. *Horatio Nelson, Viscount Nelson*, 1758–1805: Britain's most famous and colorful naval hero whose chief exploits were directed against the French.

47. *Jules Mazarin*, 1602–1661: French statesman, cardinal of the Roman Catholic Church. Mazarin learned statecraft under Cardinal Richelieu, chief minister of Louis XIII. After the king's death, Mazarin was chief minister to the regent, Anne of Austria.

49. The paper was meant to hold the tomato's shape. Unfortu-

nately, this step is not necessary with most tomatoes available today.

51. *Giacomo Meyerbeer*, 1791–1864: German composer of opera. His most successful operas were in French. Two comic operas, *L'Etoile du Nord* and *Dinorah*, were highly popular crowd pleasers.

52. *Johannes Gutenberg*, c. 1397–1468: German inventor and printer long credited with the invention of printing by movable type.

60. This very old recipe is traditionally classified with soups, although it is more like an entrée.

65. *La Rochelle*: The principal Atlantic fishing port of France, a Huguenot stronghold for fifty years.

66. *Peter the Great*, 1672–1725: Czar of Russia from 1682 to 1725. Peter remains a controversial figure for the vehemence with which he forced on his nation the habits, ways of thought, and style of western European culture.

68. *mousselines*: Made of minced chicken breast, egg white, and cream. They can be colored red with meat or carrot juice, or green with juice squeezed out of chopped parsley stems through a cloth.

71. *chantilly*: Good, thick cream suitable for whipping.
brown game puree: A puree of roast game and browned vegetables.

73. *Artois*: Region of northern France near the English Channel under Hapsburg rule from the late Middle Ages until the wars against King Louis XIV of France.

75. *Anne-Marie-Louise d'Orléans, duchesse de Montpensier*, 1627–1693: Also called La Grande Mademoiselle, niece of King Louis XIII of France. An active rebel against the Crown who led troops of her own in the nobility's fight against the power of the Crown.

76. *chicken blanquette*: An elaborate stew bound with egg and cream.

84. *baveuses*: Also found written as *Pavösen* or *Pofesen*. Sandwiches dipped in egg and grilled, like the French *croque-monsieur*.

87. The meat used in this recipe is most similar to smoked corned beef. However, smoked beef or any pork other than ham may also be used.

92. This preparation is called Japanese because it was served over rice. Toward the end of the century, things Japanese were of great interest in Vienna.

99. Reserving this pâté on ice would have given it the *haut goût* or "high taste" once valued in meat, especially game. Since this preference no longer exists, it is better to use the pâté sooner.

101. *sauce américaine*: This sauce is the product of preparing lobster with oil, tomato, onion, garlic, parsley, fish stock, and white wine. There is much uncertainty as to whether this preparation comes from America or from Armorica (Brittany), where lobster is a characteristic food.

102. *garnish à la royale*: Prepared in small cylindrical molds called *darioles* and steamed in a double boiler. When done, the custard is finely sliced. This garnish can be made in a fireproof glass form and then diced.

104. *Aleksandr Vasilyevich Suvorov*, 1729–1800: Russian field marshall who reached his peak in the French revolutionary wars of 1798–1799, in which he commanded Austro-Russian forces against the French Republic.

105. *Anthelme Brillat-Savarin*, 1755–1826: French jurist and civil servant who was banished during the Reign of Terror and spent his exile in Switzerland and the United States. His writings, concerned with law, economics, and dueling, were relatively undistinguished, but his work on gastronomy, *Physiologie du goût* (1825), is one of the best in existence.

111. *Graf Maximilian von Trauttmansdorff*, 1584–1650: Austrian diplomat and statesman, instrumental in securing the Bohemian and Hungarian crowns (1617–1618) and the imperial title for Ferdinand II. He was prime minister of Austria from 1648 to 1650.

112. *Stéphanie Clotilde Hermine Marie Charlote*, 1864–1945: Daughter of Leopold II of Belgium, wife of Rudolf, Crown Prince of Austria-Hungary.

113. *Sir Walter Scott*, 1771–1832: Scottish novelist, knighted for his vivid reconstructions of Scottish history.

115. *Pálffy*: A family prominent and powerful in Hungary for centuries. In the early eighteenth century Janos Pálffy worked earnestly to end the conflict between Austria and Hungary.

118–126. These recipes for goulash present some interesting signs of blending of Austrian and Hungarian influences. The dish and its name are originally Hungarian, originating from a simple stew made by cowherds, who are called *gulyás* in Hungarian. In Austria, goulash is eaten with a knife and fork and consists of beef, onion, and spices. In Hungary, *gulyás* is a soup, while the dish that is eaten with a knife and fork is called *pörkölt* and can be made with veal or pork as well as beef and can have potatoes in it. While people always did and still do cook goulash at home, there is no denying that the best place to eat it is in a small restaurant, possibly because it is made in larger quantities there and certainly because it is reheated a few times.

118. *Debrecen*: A city known since the thirteenth century, economic and cultural center of the great plain in the easternmost region of Hungary. It was a stronghold of Protestantism in the sixteenth century, a refuge against the Turkish invaders in the seventeenth century, and the seat of resistance to Austrian rule in the early nineteenth century.

121. *Troppau*: Now known as Opava in the Czech Republic, was founded in the twelfth century and later became the capital of Austrian Silesia. In 1820 representatives of the European powers met there at the Congress of Troppau to discuss problems arising after the settlement of the Napoleonic Wars.

122. *Count Gyula Andrássy*, 1823–1890: Hungarian politician who was one of the leading figures in the 1848–1849 Hungarian revolution. He was prominent in the negotiations leading to the Compromise of 1867, which created the Austro-Hungarian monarchy.

123. *Székely*: What people in one part of the Magyar nation, living in Translyvania, have called themselves for more than a thou-

sand years. But this goulash is not named for them. It bears the name of a restaurant owner in Szeged, the second largest city in Hungary.

124. *à la Holstein*: Designates any dish topped with a fried egg.

141. *Jeanne-Antoinette Poisson Le Normant d'Etoiles Marquise de Pompadour*, 1721–1764: Mistress and longtime confidante of King Louis XV of France. Although she was of middle-class origin, she gained success and influence in state policy because of her intelligence and capabilities. She encouraged the French alliance with Austria.

142. This turkey recipe must be from Translyvania, the only region of the empire where turkeys were prized at the time.

DESSERTS

4. *Clarify sugar*: Before boiling sugar to the degree required by a given recipe, it is necessary to prepare a syrup. If the boiling mixture is not skimmed, as directed by this recipe, sugar graining results, and the preparation will not be smooth. The clarification stage is over when the bubbles in the boiling mixture are small and very close together.

5. *sugar scale*: When sugar syrup prepared in advance is used, it is necessary to check the exact proportion of sugar and water that it contains. This can be measured on a so-called Baumé thermometer, which is graduated from 0 to 44 degrees, corresponding to degrees above the boiling point of water. The temperature at which the mixture boils indicates the extent to which the sugar has raised the boiling point and thus the sugar concentration.

11. *arrack*: A spirit distilled from fermented rice or from coconut milk or sap.

26. *chaudeau*: A sauce, usually sweet, based on hot milk.

28. *tea pastries*: These cookies were made in October and stored for winter use.
    satangali: Also called salt of staghorn. Used as a form of baking powder.

33. *Esterházy*: The Esterházy family of Galánta was one of the richest and most powerful noble lines in Hungary. At its

height, the family owned fifty marketplaces, four hundred villages, and twenty-one castles. The line produced field officers, diplomats, art collectors, and patrons of the arts. Prince Miklós József (1714–1790) was marshall of Austria; the composer Joseph Haydn was his court composer and music director. In light of the excellent magnificence of this line, it is no wonder that Austrian cuisine gives the name Esterházy to the most sumptuous dishes.

cornets: Small conical pastries, very much like an ice cream cone but finer in texture, sometimes filled with cream.

42. *potash*: Potassium carbonate, used as leavening for cakes and cookies.

54. *Sarah Bernhardt*, 1844–1923: A French actress considered the greatest romantic and classical tragic actress of her time. She was also an accomplished painter, poet, sculptor, and playwright.

59. *spun sugar*: A mixture of sugar and water that has been boiled until a drop pulled between thumb and forefinger forms threads.

63. *Baden*: The spa and resort town where Katharina Schratt was born.

70. *alcohol*: Unflavored vodka can be used for this purpose.

74. *granita*: Also called sorbet, this kind of ice is neither solid nor liquid. It is made from fruit syrups which never have a density on the Baumé scale of more than 14 degrees. Granitas are served between the main courses of a dinner.

83. *Karl Robert Graf Nesselrode*, 1780–1862: A Russian statesman of German descent who dispatched troops to help Austria crush the Hungarian revolt led by Louis Kossuth. No matter how delicious the pudding may be, it seems remarkable to find it, at least by this name, in a collection that bears so many marks of affinity with Hungary.

84. *croquembouche*: Any of several dessert preparations consisting of small objects, usually spherical, either coated with or made of something that crackles in the mouth.

brittle stage: Boiling sugar water has reached this stage when the syrup detaches itself in thin sheets from a spoon dipped in hot water and shatters like glass.

86. *Oskar Pischinger*: A well-known confectioner at the end of the nineteenth century. This recipe would have been quite fashionable at the time it was collected.
   Karlsbad wafers: A mixture of flour and water baked on an iron. They may be perfectly smooth or slightly textured.

90. *Johannisberger wine*: Probably means Riesling.

91. *Hermann Ludwig Heinrich, Fürst von Pückler-Muskau, 1785–1871*: A landscape gardener on a grand scale and the most beloved German travel writer of the mid-nineteenth century.

98. *Hohensalzburg*: An eleventh-century mountain fortress dominating the city of Salzburg. The cake is meant to be tall and imposing, like the fortress.

102. *Brabant*: A province in central Belgium which was in the possession of the Hapsburg family from the fifteenth century to the end of the eighteenth century.

105. *Ödenburg*: German name of the Hungarian city Sopron, one of the country's oldest cultural centers.

125. *Sacher*: The Hotel Sacher was founded in the second half of the nineteenth century. It has always been, and still is today, not only a hotel, restaurant, café, and bar, but also a landmark and a symbol of the best that Austria has to offer in the way of sophisticated, truly Viennese hospitality. Sachertorte was devised by the founder's father in 1835. Today, it is still being shipped around the world in elegant wooden boxes. There is unending discussion about the "right" way to make it.

131. *Trieste*: An Adriatic port under Austrian rule until 1918.

144. *Mannheim*: A major inland port at the confluence of the Rhine and Neckar Rivers. In the late eighteenth century, a great European musical and theatrical center.

BRING VIENNA TO YOUR TABLE!
Chef Louis Szathmáry

During the almost half century I have been diligently and actively collecting books, first for my own collection and later on behalf of a book-purchasing fund established under my name by Johnson & Wales University in Providence, Rhode Island, I have dealt with over seven hundred book dealers. But the late Mr. Clifford Maggs, owner and operator of Maggs Brothers of Berkeley Square, had a very special place in my mind and heart. When my wife and I took my teenage daughter to Maggs Brothers for the first time, she was the fifth generation of my family on my father's side to make the acquaintance of the firm. It was a memorable moment when Clifford Maggs told us about the account held by my great-grandfather, my grandfather, and my father, as we sat around a small desk once owned by Charles Dickens. Mr. Clifford was not only a book dealer to me but much more: a teacher, advisor, and good friend. He was extremely well versed for an Englishman in both of the fields in which I was collecting seriously: Hungarology and gastronomy. Through the years, he helped me acquire some of the finest pieces in my collection, many of them now in the library of the University of Iowa.

Perhaps the most intriguing of these is a handwritten cookbook which Mr. Clifford purchased on my behalf at an auction in London. The estate being auctioned belonged to the late Baron Kiss de Ittebe, son of an Austro-Hungarian career diplomat and the actress Katharina Schratt. Mr. Clifford found the book so interesting that he felt he could purchase it on my behalf without even consulting me. He airmailed the book to me the day after the call, and I think it needless to say that my check was already in the mail before the book arrived.

This little cookbook was perhaps the most insignificant-look-
ing object among the more than one hundred handwritten cookbooks in my collection. It was certainly not the oldest, not the
most expensive, not the best illustrated, not the best docu-
mented, but definitely the most mysterious and most intriguing.
It had no author, no title, and it contained a most peculiar group
of recipes, or rather notes, memos, suggestions, and reminders of
possibilities. It was written in fairly good but not particularly
educated German and included words in not-so-good French
and not-so-good Hungarian. The pages were definitely written
by a woman's hand, and, as far as I am concerned, it was not the
work of a cook or housekeeper. Rather, it was the work of a person who knew enough about food and entertainment to be able
to suggest and to approve a menu and give instructions when
needed. The evenness of the handwriting indicates that the
recipes were not recorded one at a time but copied in just a few
sittings. For some reason, the son of Katharina Schratt thought
enough of the book to take it along with him when he moved to
England and to keep it in his possession until the end of his life.

As soon as I acquired the book, I decided that some day, some
day soon, I would try some of the recipes, perhaps even translate them, select some for an article or for a chapter in a book, or
perhaps translate and publish the book in its entirety. Thanks
to the University of Iowa and its library, and thanks to the fore-
sight and diligence of David Schoonover, Rare Book Librarian
and Curator of the Szathmáry Family Culinary Collection at the
University of Iowa, this longtime dream is turning into a reality.
Gertrud Graubart Champe and Paula von Haimberger Arno,
both native Austrians, graciously invited me to work with them
on the practical, culinary aspects of the book. Thanks to the generous and expert cooperation of the Johnson & Wales Culinary
Archives & Museum, I had the great privilege and pleasure of
preparing dishes from almost a hundred of the recipes: baking,
cooking, frying, freezing, steaming, sautéing, and serving appe-
tizers, salads, main courses, soups, and desserts.

After reading the entire manuscript in both the original German and the translated English version, I selected recipes that I felt not only could be but should be made available in a form that the readers of this book could prepare without being professional cooks or even outstanding amateurs in the field of gastronomy. I want to bring recipes to the table for the social historians, historians, and people interested in the arts, literature, music, and entertainment of a European metropolis during the time from the 1880s to the beginning of the First World War in 1914.

This time in Austria-Hungary was an era of rapid evolution, slow revolution, upward mobility, and the mobility of migration. One could use words about the empire like creation, turmoil, ferment, elegance, but also describe it with words like conservative, stodgy, hypocritical, inequitable. But whatever Austria-Hungary was, it was strikingly visible to the rest of the world. Indeed, the periods called Victorian and Edwardian, the time from 1849 until 1916, could just as accurately be called the era of Franz Joseph I, emperor of Austria, king of Hungary, ruler of an empire both intellectually and technologically the unchallenged leader of Europe. Franz Joseph's realm enfolded many nations. Poles and Bohemians, Hungarians and Croats, Italians and Serbs lived under one ruler, one government, in one country. Lacking political autonomy, these nations yet pursued their ethnic life through culture and music, art and sciences, retaining for centuries their family customs, their ethnic costumes, their agriculture, horticulture, and animal husbandry. And all this while they were also exchanging the ethnicity and peculiarities of their food ways with ever-widening influences on each other.

One example of this kind of transfer occurred when Austrian military cooks, feeding the troops who won a war against a northern kingdom on the Apulian peninsula, learned a new way (at least to them) to prepare veal: cut it into thin slices, dip it in flour, then beaten eggs and bread crumbs, and sauté it in shortening. When this dish was first served in Vienna, it was called Milanese, then it became that famous and favorite Austrian dish, Wiener schnitzel, which also ranked as the number one national dish of Hungary at the end of World War I. After the Second

World War, a survey of Hungarian restaurants in the United States, Canada, Australia, and South America showed that more menus featured *becsi szelet* on their menus than—believe it or not—Hungarian goulash.

But Wiener schnitzel does not appear in our book, because the book is not about the food that most Viennese, whether of high or low estate, ate every day. The recipes in it are for special occasions, perhaps notes from elegant parties. For the other dishes, no recipes were needed. Katharina Schratt always had an excellent cook in the house who could make all the wonderful Viennese dishes with one hand tied behind her back. So there is no mention of creamed spinach or Tafelspitz or roast pork. But it is nice to note that two dishes, which are also very typical and beloved by all sorts of Viennese, are indeed generously represented because they are well known as Franz Joseph's favorites— goulash and gugelhupf.

These dishes as well as many others that graced Katharina's table are accessible to today's cooks. Learning how to reproduce them is really not so much a matter of technical skill, given the number of perfectly acceptable shortcuts we have at our disposal today. A much more important accomplishment, if we want to think ourselves back, is the ability to return in imagination to a time when shopping and cooking were part of the celebration of the turning cycle of the year, and the preparation and serving of food were serious matters for reasons that are very different from those we might give today.

In other words, the difference between cooking then and most cooking now lies not so much in ingredients or methods as in the spirit in which both cooks and diners approach food. In the time of Katharina Schratt, people were spending more time than we do in butcher shops and grocery shops and markets, and finally in the kitchen, not only because they had less equipment at their service than we do but because it seemed not at all remarkable to spend a great deal of time on a function around which family life and well-being were constructed. Moreover, the kind and amount of food served in a household were significant indices of a family's prosperity and status. Both in cooking and in eating, there was an acknowledgment of one's environment. People were much more directly aware of where their food came from than we are and of the changes in their menu with the passage of the seasons. But perhaps the sharpest contrast with today is the fact that so many more home cooks did not cook alone, so that the kitchen was a lively place, where serious shoptalk might alternate with cheerful gossip, and hard work was relieved by company and the antics of the youngest scullery maid.

Think about the seasons and what a difference they can make to the table. Who is better off, for instance — people who consume mediocre watermelon for thirteen months of the year or people who only eat it in hot, hot summer, spitting seeds toward the river with juice dripping from their chins? Who is richer? People who can grab cold storage apples from baseball season to baseball season or those who wait for delightful summer apples in June and wonderful baking apples in winter? And think of tomatoes . . . red, soft, generous treasure of high summer! In Europe, in tomato season, the marketplace draws people by the nose to the stands where the tomatoes are sinfully juicy and red. Is it any wonder that, in the state of Massachusetts in the late 1800s, in certain communities the local ordinance still called for a six-foot fence and a warning sign if you had tomatoes inside. Why? Because our forebears firmly believed that eating tomatoes would make you a sinner.

In the time in which this little notebook originated, people ate things in season only. The first little red radishes were celebrated just like the first large heads of cabbage. The tiny fragrant wild strawberries in the forests, the fresh ears of corn piled up at the market, and the first new potatoes were all treated by the sellers with the same delicacy required for table grapes or dates brought in from other corners of the world. In Franz Joseph's Vienna, all the foods had their day, each in its own season. The fresh vegetables, the spring chickens, the large, heavy geese of St. Martin's day in November, the first rack of venison roasted after the start of the season, all these were occasions for celebration. When the first lemonade stand opened its doors in the great park called the Prater, people lined up to buy a sweet cool glass of the fresh drink, just as they lined up at the bus stops in Vienna when the first chestnut seller started to roast his imported *castagne* in the crisp days of fall. And when, in the Viennese suburb of Grinzing, the first winegrower hung out his bunch of evergreen branches to let the world know that his new wine was ready, one of the largest cities in Europe started to move — on bicycle and by horseback, in autos and streetcars, carrying picnics to the little places on the hillsides among the vineyards where the *Heuriger* was served to the tune of accordions and fiddles and zithers playing the sweet old songs.

The spinach had to be ready, rain or shine, the week before Easter, because on Maundy Thursday, you simply have to eat spinach with a faint flavor of nutmeg and garlic, the only dish where these two tastes are combined, deepening the mysterious green flavor of fresh spinach. The newspapers would tell you when the first plum dumplings were going to appear on the handwritten menus displayed on the doors of tiny restaurants or when the first brook trout arrived in the grand outdoor restaurants along the Danube or the first fresh red raspberries arrived in the window of Demel's. There were organized street festivals for the arrival of the first large barrels of bock beer, the official drink to announce the undeniable arrival of spring. Everything had its own season . . . the snails from the vineyards, the apricots from the Wachau district on the shores of the Danube west of Vienna. In February or in July you could not buy a single stalk of asparagus in Vienna, but toward the end of April or the beginning of May, in shop windows and on stands in the open markets, asparagus was the king, no, not the king but the prince, because it couldn't be that old. Even head lettuce had its debut just like the green beans, the first young carrots, and the first walnuts in fragile and fragrant light brown shells.

And the mushrooms, all the different wild mushrooms which came to the market: egg yolk yellow, pale gray, deep brown. The different mushrooms were accompanied by different seasonal items on the menu. Certain of them were offered in creamy soft scrambled eggs with new potatoes, while others came in their own herb-scented red wine sauce or deep fried and served with fresh mayonnaise. Mushroom slices the size of a woman's hand were quickly sautéed, Italian style, in a frying pan or made into a heavenly soup served with a slice of mushroom floating on a piece of toasted roll. Mushrooms were served with chicken livers and a faint hint of garlic or with lots of onions and fresh bay leaf or many other ways, but each one only for a short season and only on mornings when the pickers who had left at 2 A.M. for their secret patches arrived at the market around 5:30 or 6:00. Even the simplest staple of the Viennese kitchen had its day. The big, clean-scrubbed barrels were pushed to market on a single-wheeled pushcart, and a cloud of the intriguing fragrance of just-finished sauerkraut was carried through the air.

But this close attention to the seasons does not mean that nothing was stored. So I will tell you about that treasure house known as the Viennese pantry. The spice rack of the Viennese housewife is a simple one but dignified. You can't imagine any kitchen without black pepper, salt, cinnamon, or parsley flakes. The herbs used by practically everybody are bay leaf, marjoram, tarragon, and white pepper. The fresh herbs are flat parsley, chive, onions, and scallions for the savory dishes, while vanilla, cinnamon, nutmeg, and mace are used for sweet ones. Garlic is not used as much as in France, but a household cannot be without it. Herbal teas such as chamomile and linden blossoms are among every housewife's treasures. Of course, paprika is an integral item in the spice collection. Otherwise, how could you make a Fiakergoulash or a good Hackbraten? Tomatoes are also used as a flavoring agent. In late summer when the vines are heavy with ripe fruit, it can be very satisfying to cook them at home and bottle them as thick, heavy juice or light sauce.

Dried fruit and nuts are needed for many dishes, and what is a pantry without dried apple slices, pitted or unpitted prunes, dried pears, dried apricots, almonds, and walnuts? Out in the country, especially in regions with forests, hazelnuts are all over the place for kids to pick up on the way home from school. Chestnuts are another staple, not in the cupboard but at the market, where certain stands sell nothing but shelled and unshelled nuts, ranging from whole coconuts to tiny sesame seeds.

What other treasures could be found in the pantry? Good things hanging from hooks in the ceiling or from rods resting across the tops of two cupboards: tulle bags of garlic, nuts, and shallots; hams and sausages; strings of mushrooms; bundles of dried herbs. On the shelves stood jars of rendered fat (*Schmalz*), pickled meat, preserves. On the floor there might be a root box, where celery root, parsley root, carrots, and potatoes were stored in sifted quartz sand. Apples were stored on straw, wine rested in racks; all the bounty of the earth lay ready to become a feast. This kind of pantry is not just a farmhouse phenomenon. It could be found in any well-managed urban middle-class kitchen. The culture of gathering food in season and storing it for future use still has echoes in Austria. A Viennese family still takes pleasure in buying a bushel of summer fruit and putting it up in rows of shiny glass jars. After all, it is a mark of civilization not to eat up all one's best food in one grand orgy.

Of all the spices and herbs to be found in a Viennese pantry, paprika always seems to be the one that has the greatest right to be there. In part this is because it provides one of the most characteristic tastes of Viennese food, but also in part it is because of the 350 years of wandering that brought it to triumph on central European tables.

In central Europe, from the Middle Ages onward, one of the most common spices was ginger. In the mid-nineteenth century came the revolutionary takeover of a red spice called paprika in many Germanic and Slavic languages, as well as in the Finno-Ugric languages. The stage for this takeover was set by Columbus, who made his voyage in part because of the great demand in Europe for pepper. This black berry, a staple of trade between Europe and India, was so costly that a few pounds of black pepper made a very suitable royal gift. Columbus, not wishing to return empty-handed from the voyage which did not take him to India, brought back different spices, also quite hot, namely the fruit of various species of *Capsicum*, the genus which includes green peppers, chilies, and cayenne peppers. These plants, relatives of potatoes, tomatoes, and the deadly nightshade, were cultivated and carried around the shores of the Mediterranean mostly by Spanish merchants, and the ground spice was called Turkish pepper. The plants spread to Slavic countries, where the ground form of milder varieties was known as paprika. By the eighteenth century, the plants were considered very desirable and could be found growing in the gardens of royalty and princes of the church. By the mid-nineteenth century, paprika had completely replaced ginger and changed the food customs not only of Hungary but of Italy, Austria, and Bohemia as well. Hardly fifty years after it had first been mentioned as a spice, Auguste Escoffier was already creating recipes with it.

Vienna was a natural place for paprika to land. This busy city was the crossroads of Europe, with rich paprika merchants from Poland and the Ukraine, scientists and artists from Prague, and composers and performers from East and West traveling up and down the Danube by ship, by coach, and, at the turn of the century, by train. Paprika began to be seen together with salt and pepper on royal dining tables and in small family restaurants in Grinzing. The Jockey Club in Vienna as well as the Sacher Hotel had to put goulash and paprikash on the menus, and the world-famous pastry shop in Bad Ischl, Zauner, started to offer afternoon tea or a glass of wine accompanied by a new type of cheese pastry sprinkled with cheese and paprika, which had taken the place of caraway seed.

🦋 THE MEALS OF AN AUSTRIAN DAY 🦋

It is hard to know whether to use the past tense or the present tense in talking about the customs surrounding food in Austria. There are still echoes today of tastes, customs, and practices of former centuries. In spite of new inventions, a new rhythm of life, and the international influence of the hamburger, food habits are conservative; they tend to be modified a bit rather than dropped.

BREAKFAST (*Frühstück*)

Breakfast might be a delicious, tiny meal, like fresh, crisp rolls, the *Kaisersemmel* with its crusty crown or *Kipferl*, yeast dough crescents, something like a croissant, that still commemorate the narrow escape from the Turkish invaders of the seventeenth century, fresh sweet butter and jam, accompanied by fragrant coffee served with a little pitcher of hot milk. Or breakfast might be a serious meal.

MENU 1
Omelette
Toasted slices of *Kaisersemmel.* In places where it is
hard to get Viennese rolls, use prebaked rolls such as
Pepperidge Farm brown-and-serve French rolls.
3 or 4 compound butters
Juice or fresh fruit

MENU 2
Egg dish with garnish
Potato dish
Bowl of chilled canned sour cherries and fresh orange slices

MENU 3
Poached egg with goose liver puree
Gugelhupf
Stewed rhubarb

BRUNCH (*Gabelfrühstück*)

Gabelfrühstück is something like a brunch. This meal, often eaten out in a café or a pub, was chiefly in a man's domain in the days when men went out to work and women stayed at home and worked.

The food consumed at *Gabelfrühstück* can be quite spicy and is often accompanied by a glass of wine or beer. In the late twentieth century, it has in some cases joined the repertory of fast foods; trucks drive around Austrian cities in the morning, delivering frozen individual portions of goulash or *Beuschel* (a stew of variety meats in a savory sauce) and dumplings to many a pub or café. *Gabelfrühstück* is a pleasant meal to prepare for company on a weekend morning.

MENU 1
Goulash à la Debrecen
Small salad or pickles
Assorted rolls, including salt sticks

MENU 2
Stuffed hard-boiled eggs decorated with caviar
Frankfurters with mustard and fresh grated horseradish
Raw sauerkraut
Fresh fruit

MENU 3
Poultry rice with Parmesan cheese
Bibb lettuce salad
Peeled sliced oranges with another fresh fruit, laced with
orange liqueur or nonalcoholic syrup

DINNER (*Mittagessen*)

The main meal comes in the middle of the day. It consists of four courses and represents the best of the good housewife's ability to plan, shop, and cook (or supervise the cook).

MENU 1
Soup à la Rohan
Ground meat dumplings
Potatoes
Beet salad
Poppy seed strudel

MENU 2

Beef soup

Goulash à la Debrecen

Macaroni or spaetzle or potatoes

Carrots in dill sauce

Vanilla crescents

MENU 3

Soup à la Pierre le Grand

Fillet à la Trauttmansdorff

Boston bibb or Kentucky limestone bibb lettuce salad

Piquant fruit

TEA (*Jause*)

At four or five o'clock in the afternoon, it is time for coffee and cake or some savory pastry. This is a cozy meal, a nice time to invite friends or family for a visit.

SUPPER (*Nachtmahl*)

Later on in the evening came supper. It was a simpler meal than the four-course noon meal but still included a hot dish. Sometimes it consisted, as it still does today, of a bowl of soup and a hot, starchy dessert, which is so characteristic of Viennese at-home cooking.

MENU 1

Omelette provençale

Mixed green salad with vinaigrette

Buttered toast

MENU 2

Consommé with forcemeat quenelles

Noodles à la Ödenburg

Oranges

Stuffed baked potato
Watercress salad with vinaigrette or light sour cream dressing
Fruit and cheese of leftover pastry from lunch

FORMAL DINNER (*Diner*)

Oysters on the half-shell
Clear chicken soup with mousselines
Hungarian stuffed cabbage
Roast capon with poached fruit (apricots, peaches,
or canned quince apples)
Roast potato
Green salad with hard-boiled eggs and raw mushrooms
Cheese (Austrian or German or French), dark rye or
pumpernickel bread, radishes
Torte

EVENING PARTY (*Imbiß*)

After struggling for a long time to define this meal in English, I
came to the conclusion that to understand it, one must think of
it as an event which allows for great variety and occasionally per-
mits the good cook to use items that are already available in the
refrigerator. In other words, it's "clean the ice-box," but with
flair. Prepare a generous buffet with these ideas in mind:

Roast: Roast pork or roast beef or any other cooked meat or
fish can be sliced and arranged on a platter. Serve with a variety of mustards and other bottled sauces.
Savories: Choose six to eight different small dishes from
among the small sandwiches, canapés, croustades. Add one or
two pâtés and perhaps some other savory dishes.
Cold Cuts: Offer several types of cheese and good European
sausages such as Hildesheimer or Braunschweiger liverwurst,
ring bologna, smoked tongue, smoked pork loin, Genoa or

Hungarian salami. Add a stuffed egg dish, prepared from poulet eggs or Grade A small eggs. If you use a larger size, cut the eggs into four pieces instead of two.

Vegetables: Roll thinly sliced ham around white or green asparagus; fill cherry tomatoes, large gooseberries, or tiny potato balls with creamed avocado, strong cheese (Roquefort, Stilton, Danish blue, creamed with butter). Offer a variety of sliced fresh vegetables, including sticks of young, fresh celery root and kohlrabi.

Breads: Serve a variety of breads, slices of rolls. Make melba toast by slicing any kind of bread thin and rebaking it at 275 degrees until it is golden and very dry but not brown.

Sweets: Choose two or three cakes or tortes and two or three small pastries or cookies.

❧ THE RECIPES ❧

As we have seen, Katharina Schratt's kitchen notebook has the sound of a knowledgeable woman talking to herself and her cook. We are separated from that cook by a wide river of time, materials, methods, and attitudes about food. And yet it is by no means impossible to come very close to the taste for which Katharina's cook was universally praised. After all, some of the very complicated methods associated with nineteenth-century cooking are not wonderful in themselves but are hardworking substitutes for various technologies that, for better or worse, we have at our disposal today. Never forget that people don't eat methods; they enjoy results. The recipes that follow are adapted for the modern kitchen. They also take modern taste into account, since indigestion is a very high price to pay for authenticity.

Most of the recipes presented here are modernized or interpreted versions of recipes found in our collection. Some, however, were not mentioned there and are presented in order to offer a more complete picture of the Austrian kitchen. These added dishes are so much a part of the Viennese taste that they are completely taken for granted. In fact, someone who could not make the vegetables presented here or the Tafelspitz, for instance, without looking into a cookbook would probably not be allowed to set foot in the kitchen at all. All the recipes, with only one or two exceptions, have been published in one or the other of my cookbooks and have been very well received by a wide public. If you choose your menu well, and if you follow these recipes with real enjoyment and enthusiasm, you will be able to recapture something of the hospitality that Katharina Schratt offered her friends.

Some words on ingredients. As you pre-read these recipes, and that is a very necessary step, you may be tempted to say that you can't get many of these ingredients and just give up, but perhaps you shouldn't. Supermarkets have widened their scope considerably, and things that were impossible to find ten years ago, or even two years ago, are there at your fingertips. Other items, things that can be shipped preserved, vacuum packed, or frozen, can be obtained easily and reliably from mail order houses cited in the List of Vendors.

CONTENTS

ANCHOVY EGGS

Hard-boiled eggs
Anchovy butter
Caviar
Parsley

Hard-boiled eggs are halved lengthwise. The rounded underside is trimmed so that the egg will stand. With a pastry bag form a wreath of anchovy butter around the yolks. In the center place a teaspoon of caviar. Decorate with parsley.

FOUR KINDS OF BREAKFAST BUTTER

About Compound Butters

In the modern kitchen, use a food processor, blender, or electric beater. Whip butter at room temperature, then start adding other ingredients, a little at a time. Instead of smoked eel, anchovy or any smoked fish such as salmon, whitefish, trout, or even canned fish may be used. Try butter made with smoked oysters from the can, with salt and lemon juice.

As a rule, use not more than three or four herbs in the same compound. Be careful that they do not clash or overpower each other. Curly parsley is a great beginning. Add flat leaf parsley, chives, shallots, or even leek, and then highlight flavor with one other herb such as basil, tarragon (either French or Russian), dill, cilantro, or your favorite, be it oregano, marjoram, paprika, or mustard. Avoid really exotic herbs even if you like them. Compound butters made with honey or good jams or jellies are also successful. Usually, compound butters are used as a first layer in a sandwich.

Vienna or French bread
Truffle butter
Herb butter
Anchovy butter
Plain butter

Spread slices of crisp bread with these butters. The plain butter is more delicious if it is unsalted.

FINE SANDWICHES
Butter
Goose liver
Eel, finely chopped
1 sardine
1 anchovy
Mustard
Paprika
Lemon juice
Caviar
White toast

Butter and goose liver are passed through a sieve. Finely chopped eel or other smoked fish, such as salmon or whitefish, is mixed with one sardine and one anchovy. Season the mixture with mustard, paprika, and lemon juice. Spread on small pieces of white toast. Decorate the sandwiches with one of the ingredients or with caviar. Finish each sandwich with a slice of olive and a slice of radish or a tiny wedge of lemon or a sprig of parsley.

STUFFED BREAD
1/2 pound butter
1/4 pound ham finely minced
1/4 pound tongue
2 hard boiled eggs
5 anchovies
1 rounded teaspoon capers
Mustard
1 loaf bread, unsliced

Scoop out the loaf of bread. Beat 1/2 pound butter until fluffy. Mince finely 1/4 pound ham, 1/4 pound tongue, 2 hard-boiled eggs, 5 anchovies, a rounded teaspoon capers, rinsed. Add mustard and the bread removed from the center of the loaf and mix all this with the beaten butter. Fill the loaf with the mixture. Store in a cold place, wrapped firmly in plastic wrap or a towel, then serve sliced.

CROUSTADES

The general term croustade covers many different things, but it is nothing more or less than a crust to surround something soft. Various kinds of crusts can be bought prebaked. In addition, there are several ways to make your own croustades from scratch or almost from scratch. One excellent dough for croustades is cream cheese dough:

12 ounces flour (3 cups)
8 ounces butter (2 sticks)
8 ounces cream cheese
1 egg
1 tablespoon water

In a large, cold bowl, mix the flour, butter, and cream cheese, working very quickly, until the mixture looks like coarse cornmeal. Press into a ball, then divide it into two portions. Wrap each portion in plastic and refrigerate for at least 3 to 4 hours.

You must mix the dough with your hands, and you must be sure that they are not hot. Have on hand a container of ice water and chill your hands on its surface. Be sure they do not get wet.

When you drop the sticks of butter and slab of cream cheese

into the flour, cover their entire surfaces with flour before you touch them. Then break the sticks of butter in two and dip the broken surfaces into the flour. Break the pieces of butter again and dip again in flour. Then start breaking the cream cheese, dipping in flour. Keep repeating this procedure, never touching the same piece of butter or cream cheese twice in succession. When all the pieces are the size of an almond, put both hands on the bottom of the mixing bowl and turn the whole mixture over. Press the mixture together with the fingertips, working quickly and running thumbs from the little finger to the index finger in a circular motion. Work the dough lightly until it can be rolled out. Line greased tartlet pans with the dough, brush it with a wash made of the egg and water, and bake in a moderate oven until golden. After two or three tries, you will master this dough, and you will find that you can roll it and fold it once, twice, or three times as you would the famous puff paste. This dough, however, is much quicker, easier, and more economical and does not require as much skill. If you do not wish to make this dough, you may take thick slices of good bread, cut out little rounds or squares, and toast them. With a small knife hollow out a depression in the toast and brush with melted butter. Toast again and fill with the desired filling.

LITTLE CROUSTADES À LA COLBERT
Croustades
Chicken puree
Plover eggs
Fill croustades with chicken puree and top with plover eggs.

CHICKEN PUREE
For 4 portions grill, broil, or pan fry an approximately 8-ounce skinless, boneless chicken breast rubbed in Chef's Salt and a pinch of white pepper. Cool and cut in half-inch cubes. Put in blender, add 2 to 3 tablespoons heavy cream, and puree. If you wish you may add some flavoring, such as 1/2 teaspoon chicken soup base or pinch of poultry seasoning or nutmeg or some finely chopped shallot or some chopped sautéed sweet onion (vidalia).

LITTLE CROUSTADES À LA STRASBOURG
Croustades
Goose liver puree
Sautéed goose liver
Demi-glaze

Fill croustades with goose liver puree, decorate with sautéed goose liver, and cover with demi-glaze.

LITTLE CROUSTADES À LA DAUPHINE
Croustades
Forcemeat dumplings
Diced truffles
Béchamel sauce

Fill croustades with a mixture of forcemeat dumplings and cubed truffles and top with a fine white sauce.

PLOVER EGGS À LA ROHAN
Croustades
Champignon puree
Quail or plover eggs

Fill croustades with champignon puree and top with plover eggs.

CHAMPIGNON PUREE
Champignons are the common white mushrooms available in the market year round. You should always make a point of using the freshest mushrooms available. They are best when the rim of the cap, on the underside of the mushroom, is still tight and close to the stem.

2 tablespoons flour
1 pound mushrooms
2 tablespoons butter (or 1 tablespoon corn oil
and 1 tablespoon butter)
1/2 teaspoon salt
generous grinding black pepper
2 or 3 tablespoons heavy cream or 1 teaspoon cornstarch and
1 teaspoon flour with 2–3 tablespoons milk (optional)
Some finely chopped parsley and a dash of brandy (optional)

Fill a large bowl with water and sprinkle the flour on the surface. Put one pound of mushrooms into the water, gently, one by one. They will bounce around and you can see the flour picking up the impurities as you rub them gently. Quickly remove the mushrooms and rinse for a few seconds under running water. Spread them out on a towel, gather the four corners, and swing the mushrooms until they are dry. Chop by hand or machine until the pieces are no larger than a peanut. Melt the shortening in a frying pan. Heat over medium heat, add the mushrooms and cover immediately to avoid spattering. Lower the heat, after about 2 minutes add 1/2 teaspoon salt, a good grinding of black pepper, and sauté for 6 to 8 minutes. You can use the mixture as it is or make a sauce: Add 2 or 3 tablespoons heavy cream or make a slurry of 1 teaspoon cornstarch and 1 teaspoon flour in 2 to 3 tablespoons milk. (In order to avoid lumps, add the liquid to the solids, not vice versa, and mix with a whip.) Add this mixture to the mushrooms and leave on the heat, stirring until it thickens. If you wish, you may add some finely chopped parsley and a dash of brandy or an herb. Depending on the desired consistency, you may chop the mushrooms until they are no larger than grains of rice, or you can make the puree smooth, like a cream. For many preparations, a somewhat coarser mixture retains the aroma better and gives an extra taste sensation because of the many surfaces touching the tongue.

RUSSIAN PATTY SHELLS

Finely cut ham

Roux

1 heaping tablespoon flour

1 tablespoon shortening (corn oil, rendered ham fat, or butter)

Cream (for 1 cup ham, use 2 to 3 tablespoons cream)

A pinch of pepper

Flat puff pastry (purchased) cut into rectangles

Cut ham fairly fine, make a roux, add the ham, pour cream and a little pepper over the mixture, cool. Cut rectangles of puff pastry with a pastry wheel, fill with the mixture, and fold into triangles. If flat frozen puff pastry is not available in your supermarket, you may fill frozen patty shells or croustades with the same mixture. Bake according to package instructions.

PATTY SHELLS À LA DAUPHINE

Patty shells
Forcemeat quenelles
Diced truffles
Béchamel sauce

Fill patty shells with forcemeat dumplings and diced truffles. Top with sauce and bake at 325 degrees or according to package directions.

FORCEMEAT QUENELLES

3/4 pound round of veal
2 slices white bread without crust, softened in a little water
2 eggs
Butter
Salt
Nutmeg
1 egg yolk
A little milk

Put 3/4 pound round of veal through a meat grinder at least three times. Combine the softened white bread and 2 eggs, sautée in butter until the mixture looks like scrambled eggs. After this mixture has cooled, mix with the meat, add salt and nutmeg, and press through a sieve. Then add one yolk and a little milk and form quenelles the size of an almond or a walnut. Add them one by one to water that is almost boiling (200 to 205 degrees) and lightly salted. Simmer 8–10 minutes if small, 10–12 minutes if larger.

Note: These dumplings can be used as a light meat course by making them larger and less finely ground.

FRANKFURTERS

The frankfurters that taste the most like the well-loved *Wiener-würstl* are those with a natural casing. Miniature cocktail sausages or miniature Bavarian or white wurst are also a good solution. Steam the sausages and bring to the table in a nice covered dish with just a very little bit of water in the bottom to prevent drying out. Offer this with a good mustard or mustard sauce, freshly grated raw horseradish or a good bottled horseradish, and rinsed raw sauerkraut as side dishes. Serve the sausages with salt sticks, either homemade or from a bakery, or with excellent seeded rye bread.

PHEASANT PÂTÉ
Roast pheasant
Pâté spice
Stock
Sauce espagnole
Salt
Pepper
Bacon

Bone out the roast pheasant. Rub the breast with salt and pâté spice and set aside. With the rest of the meat and some bacon, prepare a finely ground forcemeat. Simmer the bones in water and stock until the liquid is well reduced; use this to thin the sauce espagnole. Add the sauce to the forcemeat and season with salt, pepper, and pâté spice. Line a tureen or a mold with bacon, cover with forcemeat, place the breast pieces in the center. Cover with more forcemeat and bacon. Steam for 3 hours in a moderate oven. Set tureen on ice and serve cold. When cold, this pâté may be unmolded and served sliced.

ROAST PHEASANT
2 large pheasants
2 teaspoons salt
1/2 teaspoon black pepper
1/4 teaspoon juniper berries
1/2 teaspoon paprika
3 or 4 carrots, coarsely chopped
1 large onion, coarsely chopped

2 or 3 stalks of celery, coarsely chopped
2 bay leaves
Bacon
2 to 3 cups water
4 to 6 tablespoons melted shortening, preferably lard
or bacon drippings

Preheat oven to 325 to 350 degrees. If your pheasants are frozen, be sure that they are fully thawed.

Rub the pheasants with a mixture of the salt, black pepper, crushed juniper berries, and paprika. Place the coarsely chopped vegetables and the bay leaves in the bottom of a deep roasting pan large enough to hold the pheasant. Lay the birds on the vegetables breast-side down and brush the skin with the melted shortening. Add the water to the roasting pan, cover, and place in the oven. Roast for approximately 2 hours.

Note: Juniper berries are often unavailable in food markets, but ask in ethnic pharmacies. You can buy as much as a pound at one time and keep them for years; they are not like other spices that rapidly lose their pungency. Be sure to crack them gently with a mallet in the corner of a kitchen towel before using. If for some reason you can't get any juniper berries, use an ounce of gin for each bird.

SOUPS

SOUP À LA ROHAN

10 cups beef, chicken, or veal stock
Celery root
Carrots
Peas
Chervil
Forcemeat, made of game if possible

To 10 cups of a strong broth, add cutouts of boiled celery root, carrot. Add peas and chopped chervil. Serve with toast spread with game forcemeat, such as pheasant pâté.

SOUP À LA PIERRE LE GRAND

Champignon puree
4 tablespoons flour
4 tablespoons butter
4 cups white stock or canned chicken broth
Forcemeat quenelles

Make a roux of butter and flour. Dilute with 4 cups of white stock or chicken broth. Add to this soup 2 to 4 cups mushroom puree blended to complete smoothness. The resulting soup is thickened with a mixture of three egg yolks and 1/2 cup cream. To avoid curdling, mix a small amount of hot stock into the egg and cream mixture, stirring thoroughly, then pour this mixture into the hot stock, stirring as you pour. Do not allow the soup to boil after this point. Decorate the soup with forcemeat quenelles.

SOUP À L'ORLÉANS
Consommé
White and red forcemeat quenelles
Peas
Rice

Decorate consommé with white and red forcemeat quenelles, peas, and rice.

CONSOMMÉ

2-1/2 quarts beef stock or 4 cans beef consommé
(10-1/2 ounces) with 4 cans cold water
2 egg whites
1 pound lean ground beef
1 carrot, finely grated
1 tablespoon unsalted butter
1 teaspoon cornstarch
1 cup cold water
Dry sherry or Marsala wine, to taste

Pour beef stock into a large pot. Beat egg whites until frothy and mix thoroughly with the ground beef. Add this mixture, spoonful by spoonful, to the beef stock, stirring after each addition so that the meat particles separate.

Sauté the grated carrot in the unsalted butter. Drain off any remaining fat and add carrot to the meat mixture.

Mix the cornstarch with cold water. Bring the soup to a boil over medium heat, stirring with a wire whip every 4 or 5 minutes. Slowly add the cornstarch mixture, stirring constantly. Bring the soup to a boil again, lower the heat, and let it bubble slowly for 1 hour. Remove from heat, cover the pot, and let it stand for at least another hour.

Skim off as much fat as possible and, without stirring, pour the warm soup into another pot through a wet kitchen towel or several layers of cheesecloth. Do not try to pour out the meat at the bottom.

When ready to serve, reheat the soup, but be careful not to bring it to a boil. Add a few tablespoons of the wine.

The ground beef mixed with egg whites makes an excellent

meat pudding. Combine it with the yolks of 2 eggs, 4 slices of white bread soaked in milk and squeezed out, salt, pepper, and freshly chopped parsley. Steam in a shallow dish in a water bath until it sets.

MOUSSELINES

8 ounces raw chicken breast, skinless and boneless
4 egg whites
1 pint heavy cream or whipping cream
1 quart water, lightly salted
1/8 teaspoon nutmeg
1/2 teaspoon salt

Cut the chicken breasts into 1/2-inch cubes. Grind the meat twice with the finest blade of a meat grinder. Add the nutmeg, salt, half the egg whites, and half the cream. Add half the chicken and puree the mixture until it turns into a frothy, pale substance. Add the remaining egg whites, chicken, and cream. Blend on highest speed until the mixture resembles overwhipped heavy cream. Chill the mixture in the coldest part of your refrigerator for at least 30 minutes.

The mousselines can be colored to add interest to the presentation. To color them orange: Using a fork, mix thoroughly the white of one medium egg and 3 tablespoons of finely grated carrot. Wet a clean kitchen towel and press the mixture through it by folding the four corners of the cloth and squeezing the liquid into a cup or saucer so that the tiny pieces of carrot remain in the cloth but the orange-colored egg white goes through. To color the mousselines red, follow the same procedure, using beets; to color them green, follow this procedure, using finely chopped parsley. The mousselines may also be colored by using food coloring.

In a shallow pan, bring to a gentle boil approximately 1 quart of lightly salted water. Dip a tablespoon into the boiling water and use it to take from the mousseline preparation an amount about the size of an unshelled almond. Gently slide it into the water. Repeat until you have eight to ten mousselines.

Increase the heat slightly until the mousselines begin to puff.

They will grow to double their original size. Remove from water, drain, and repeat until all batter is used.

It is advisable to cook one mousseline and then taste it for saltiness before cooking more. You can then correct the seasoning by adding more salt if needed. If you want to make the mousselines beforehand, they must be kept submerged in warm water at approximately 160 to 170 degrees until serving time. Do not try to keep them in the stock because they will lose their beautiful snow-white color. For a variation, add fine slivers of tender ham to the mousseline preparation before poaching.

SOUP À LA ROCHELLE
10 cups stock or broth
Artichoke hearts
Asparagus tips

The broth used for this soup may be chicken, beef, or veal. Decorate with asparagus tips and cutouts made of artichoke bottoms.

WHITE RAGOUT SOUP
2 cups chicken stock or canned chicken broth or water
2 cups minced onion
4 tablespoons butter
1 clove garlic, mashed with 2 teaspoons salt
2-pound chicken, cut up
1 bay leaf
2 teaspoons tarragon
2 teaspoons sugar
1 cup white wine
1/3 cup vinegar
2 tablespoons chopped flat-leaf parsley
1/2 pound mushrooms
1-1/2 cups milk
4 tablespoons flour
1 cup sour cream

Sauté onions in butter until transparent. Mash the garlic and salt together with the flat surface of a knife until mixture turns to a pulp. Add this mixture to the onions, then add chicken, bay leaf, tarragon, sugar, white wine, vinegar, 2 cups liquid, and 2 table-spoons chopped parsley. Adjust heat to medium. Cover and cook until chicken is tender, 30 to 40 minutes. Add mushrooms and cook 2 to 3 minutes. Mix milk and flour and add to chicken. Correct seasoning if necessary. Just before serving, mix the sour cream into the soup and add remaining parsley.

SOUP À LA MONTPENSIER

White ragout soup

Round forcemeat quenelles

Steamed rice

Garnish white ragout soup with round forcemeat quenelles and steamed rice.

VEGETABLES

PAN-ROASTED POTATOES

2 pounds potatoes

3 tablespoons lard

1 tablespoon paprika

1/2 teaspoon black peppercorns

3 tablespoons butter

2 teaspoons salt

2 tablespoons finely chopped parsley

1 tablespoon caraway seeds

Wash and peel the potatoes, then wash them again. Cut them into uneven cubes, approximately 1 inch each. Place them in a large pot with enough water to cover plus one inch. Add the caraway seeds and 1 teaspoon of the salt. Bring the potatoes and liquid to a boil over medium heat. As soon as the water starts to boil, remove the pan from the fire and let stand for 5 minutes. Pour off the water, place the potatoes in a bowl, and let them stand at room temperature until cooled. Combine the remaining salt, black pepper, and paprika.

Place the butter and lard in a large, heavy frying pan. Add the cold potatoes and sprinkle the top with the salt mixture.

Place the cold frying pan containing the cold shortening and potatoes over medium heat and heat it slowly, turning the potatoes gently with a spatula once in a while. Fry until the potatoes heat through and start to turn a light golden brown color.

Remove to a serving dish. Sprinkle the potatoes with the chopped parsley and serve.

If you precook the potatoes according to the directions, the 1-inch cubes will be just barely cooked and will not have raw centers. If you should immediately start to fry them without cooling to room temperature, they would become overcooked and would break. If you let them cool and slowly reheat them, they will be piping hot but not overcooked.

The paprika will give the potatoes a beautiful golden color with only a fraction of the amount of shortening that would otherwise be needed to achieve this color. Potatoes prepared in this way will not be greasy and will retain the real potato taste.

RICE SAUSAGES
2 cups rice
cooked in 4 cups of milk
1/2 teaspoon salt
2–3 cups bread crumbs (see appendix)
1–1-1/2 cups shortening for frying (peanut or corn oil)

Cook rice according to package directions, using milk instead of water. Add salt and allow the rice to cool. Form little sausages out of the rice, then bread and fry them.

SWABIAN SPAETZLE
3 cups flour
4 eggs
1 cup milk
1 teaspoon salt
4 to 6 tablespoons butter

Fill a large pot about two-thirds full with water. Add approximately 1 teaspoon salt for each quart of water used. Cover and bring the water to a boil, then set the heat so the water remains at a gentle boil.

With a fork, beat the eggs with the milk.

In a large mixing bowl, combine the flour and salt with the beaten egg mixture. Stir with a wooden spoon until the batter is smooth and all the flour is incorporated. Pour about one-third of the dough onto a dinner plate which you can easily hold up near the pot of boiling water. Dipping the tablespoon into the water each time, to prevent sticking, spoon the dough into the boiling water, taking an amount about the size of an almond each time. Continue until all the dough is used.

Cover the pot three-quarters of the way, leaving an opening so that the steam and foam which develop as the spaetzle cook can escape. Stir once in a while. Cook until all the spaetzle are on top of the water. Test one of the larger spaetzle by cutting through it to be sure that no raw center remains.

Pour into a colander and immediately rinse very quickly and briefly with cold water. Shake as dry as possible.

Place the dumplings in a frying pan and distribute the butter over the top. Let it melt, then gently turn the spaetzle with a spatula and keep them warm until served.

Do not overwork the dough, as this will result in hard, chewy spaetzle.

CREAMED SPINACH

2 pounds fresh or 2 12-ounce packages frozen spinach
2 slices white bread, crusts removed
1 cup milk
Freshly ground black pepper to taste
1 teaspoon salt
2 tablespoons flour
1 cup chicken broth or water
1 small clove garlic
1 egg

Soak the slices of bread in the milk. Place the washed spinach leaves in a large amount of lightly salted boiling water. Cook for 5 minutes. Drain and cool by rinsing with cold water. Shake dry. If frozen spinach is used, prepare it according to package directions. Chop the spinach very fine, by hand, using a large French knife on a wooden board.

Mash the white bread soaked in the milk. Add the egg.

Mash the garlic with the 1 teaspoon salt. Stir the flour and the garlic-salt mixture into the chicken broth or water.

Rinse a large saucepan with cold water. Do not dry. Heat the cooked spinach over medium heat until it starts to bubble and the bubbles break with a sound as they rise. Add the chicken broth or water mixture, stirring vigorously with a wooden spoon or wire whip. Adjust the heat to low and cook the mixture, covered, for 10 minutes, stirring once in a while.

Before serving, stir in the milk and bread mixture. Correct the seasoning, if necessary, with salt and black pepper. Serve.

If you grind the spinach through a meat grinder or a food mill, all of the liquid will come out and only the fibers will remain. When the leaves are chopped by hand, the knife cuts through only the cells directly under the edge of the knife, without pressing the others to remove all the juice.

The milk-soaked bread thickens the spinach and adds a mild filler which heightens the spinach flavor. If you used enough flour to thicken the spinach without the bread, the flavor would be floury.

CARROTS WITH DILL IN CREAM SAUCE

4 cups thinly sliced, fresh young carrots
1 cup water
2 tablespoons butter
1 tablespoon salt
1/2 teaspoon sugar
1/8 teaspoon white pepper
2 tablespoons flour
1 cup heavy cream
3 tablespoons freshly chopped dill weed

Place the carrots, water, butter, salt, sugar, and white pepper in a heavy saucepan. Bring the liquid to a rapid boil and cook until the carrots are tender.

Stir the flour into the heavy cream.

When the carrots are tender, pour the liquid off into another saucepan. Bring this liquid to a boil; then, stirring constantly, add the flour-cream mixture. Simmer the sauce slowly 10 to 15 minutes. After the sauce has cooked, add the freshly chopped dill and the carrot slices. Hold in a warm place for at least 15 minutes before serving.

The amount of moisture in carrots varies, depending on where they are purchased and on their freshness. It is easy to adjust the liquid in the recipe after cooking. If there is too much, simply discard some; if not enough, add a small amount of water. To test the water content of carrots, bend one before cutting or slicing. If the carrot is easy to bend and slow to go back to its original shape, the moisture level is very low; if it snaps with a noise when bent or cut and splits in a lengthwise direction, it is oversaturated with water.

For a lighter sauce, substitute 2 tablespoons cornstarch for the flour.

Fresh dill weed or tender young dill leaves are sold in season and may be frozen for a year-round supply. Holding the dill by the stem ends, dip a bunch in boiling water for 2 or 3 seconds. Immediately place in ice water to chill. Shake out some of the water but leave the bunch moist. Roll very tightly in aluminum foil and freeze. Once frozen, pack the aluminum-wrapped rolls in a plastic bag and store in the coldest part of your freezer. The dill will stay fresh for as long as a year. To use the frozen dill, remove it from the freezer just before it is needed. With a sharp knife, slicing crosswise, cut as much as needed. Repack and freeze the rest immediately.

BEET SALAD

Beets can be bought fresh, boiled gently in salted water, then cooled, peeled, and sliced, or you can buy them canned and sliced. If you use canned beets, rinse well before marinating. Beet salad, as a rule, is served without oil—just a mixture of water and vinegar at the strength of your preference, and flavored with freshly grated horseradish, caraway, bay leaf, salt and pepper, and sugar, depending on the sweetness of the beets. Sometimes the cooked beets are mixed with finely minced or thin-sliced raw onions.

BIBB LETTUCE SALAD
Boston bibb lettuce (1 head for 2 servings)
or Kentucky bibb lettuce (1 head per serving)
4 to 6 tablespoons fresh oil

1 clove garlic
Freshly ground black pepper
Pinch salt
Pinch sugar
Juice of half a lemon plus 2 tablespoons water

Sprinkle the bottom of a wooden salad bowl with salt. Cut the garlic in half and gently rub it on the salt; then discard the garlic.

Add the sugar and a little black pepper to the bowl. Pour in the oil. Then, with a fork or wire whip, dissolve the seasonings in the oil.

Pour in the lemon juice–water mixture, stirring constantly. Pour the mixture from the bowl into another container. Keep at room temperature.

Very quickly wash and dry the lettuce. Remove the outside leaves if necessary, then place the lettuce in the wooden bowl and chill.

Just before serving, vigorously stir the dressing and pour it over the salad. Toss gently and serve immediately.

If you chill the dressing or chill the lettuce with the dressing on it, the oil will become firm and separate and will not coat as nicely as when kept at room temperature.

APPLE HORSERADISH

4 medium-sized apples
2 tablespoons butter
6 tablespoons sugar
2 pinches of salt
2-by-1-inch piece of lemon rind
1 cup loosely packed, freshly grated horseradish or
1 tablespoon jarred horseradish
Juice of half a lemon

If possible, select 2 tart and 2 sweet apples, such as 2 Granny Smiths and 2 Jonathans or 2 Winesaps and 2 Golden Delicious. Core and peel the apples. Put the peelings, cores, and seeds in a small pot with 4 tablespoons sugar and cover the mixture with water. Simmer over medium heat.

Cut each apple into small, uneven pieces and put them in a

small, heavy pan with 2 tablespoons butter, 2 tablespoons sugar, no more than 2 to 3 tablespoons water, a pinch of salt, a 2-inch by 1-inch piece of lemon rind. Cover the pan and cook the apples over medium-slow heat stirring once every 2 to 3 minutes.

Your apple syrup, cooked from the peelings and cores, should now be ready. Strain it into a small container, pressing as much of the solids into the syrup as possible, and discard the rest. Start to add the syrup in small amounts to the cooking apples until the apples get really soft. Perhaps you will have to add a little more sugar, depending on the apples you chose. Remove the pan from the heat, add approximately 1 cup of loosely packed, freshly grated horseradish, the juice of half a lemon, and a pinch of salt. If you are not using fresh horseradish, add approximately 1 table-spoon of the jarred product. Be careful — some are beastly hot.

BREAD DUMPLINGS

1 quart 1/2-inch-thick bread cubes made from day-old
French, Italian, or Vienna bread
3 tablespoons butter
2 tablespoons bacon drippings or lard
3 cups flour
3 eggs
1 cup scalded milk
1 teaspoon salt
Fresh black pepper (optional)

Place 2 tablespoons of the butter and the bacon drippings or lard in a large skillet. Toast the bread cubes in this shortening.

Mix the flour with the salt in a deep bowl.

To the hot milk add the remaining butter. Pour this mixture slowly into the bowl with the dry ingredients, stirring constantly.

As the mixture starts to cool, break in the eggs. Keep stirring until all ingredients are incorporated.

Beat with a wooden spoon, adding a little warm water if nec-essary, until the mixture turns into a smooth dough somewhat stiffer than ordinary pancake batter.

Fold in the bread cubes. Sprinkle with a little pepper if desired.

With wet palms, form 16 dumplings and drop them into a pot

filled two-thirds full with slightly salted boiling water. Cook for approximately 10 minutes after you drop the last dumpling into the water.

Remove the pot from the heat and let the dumplings steam for another 3 to 5 minutes. Remove the dumplings with a slotted spoon and sprinkle them with melted butter or lard, or spoon some sour cream over them, depending on what they will be served with. This basic recipe may be varied by the addition of finely chopped sautéed onion or parsley. Be sure the pot you use is large enough to allow the dumplings to move freely. If it is not, cook only half of them at a time.

TAFELSPITZ

The cuisine of every nation has one dish which is not so much a dish, or a meal, as an event. Say the word and citizens understand at once. If you mention the word Tafelspitz to an Austrian, especially to a Viennese, the face will mellow to a pleasant smile, the eyes will shine like Christmas lights, and the nostrils will flare ever so slightly, yearning nostalgically for a whiff of the stuff that folk poetry is made of.

Tafelspitz is the name of a small cut of beef which most Americans can't even locate on the carcass, not even most butchers, unless by chance they know something about the Austrian way of cutting meat. This morsel is not an expensive piece anywhere in the world except in Vienna, where, properly prepared, it is believed to be the most festive and satisfying meat dish in the repertory. Even in Austria, Tafelspitz is prepared with other cuts of meat as well, sometimes by preference and sometimes because there is just not enough of the "real thing" to go around. The closest cut to the taste, texture, and quality that can regularly be obtained in this country is fresh beef brisket. You may want to

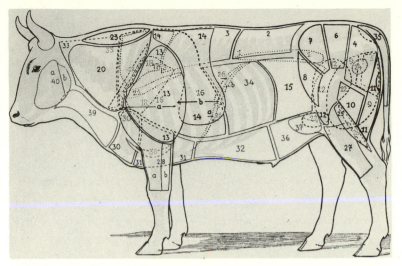

Every complete Austrian cookbook has a diagram like this, showing the Austrian way of butchering beef. The cut known as Tafelspitz is labeled number 4. Cuts 5, 6, 7, and 8 will also serve well for preparing this dish.

plan ahead and work with your butcher to find the best solution. Try bringing a chart of Austrian beef cuts with you. You may also want the butcher's help in choosing the other cuts of meat required for this recipe.

When it comes to preparing the meal, count on 5–6 hours between the final check of all ingredients and the time you call your guests to the table. If you think you will be ready in a shorter time, I am afraid you are fooling yourself. Keep in mind the side dishes and condiments you will be serving with this feast: creamed spinach, one other Viennese-style vegetable, apple horseradish, and pan-roasted potatoes. You will also want on the table: two kinds of mustard, one French, like Grey Poupon, one Austrian- or Bavarian-style, freshly grated horseradish, horseradish from the jar, and a good crackling French or Vienna bread and butter.

Your ingredients are all on hand, you have found a generous-sized roasting pan (not a stockpot) in which to prepare the Tafelspitz, and you are ready to go.

In preparing this dish, please keep in mind that careless culinary talk might call Tafelspitz boiled beef. But boiling has to do with vigorous bubbling in the cooking liquid, and this is something that must not occur when preparing Tafelspitz.

4 −5 pounds fresh brisket of beef (for this dish, you will want a total of 6 −8 ounces of meat for each person)

A piece of boneless shank meat (approximately 2 −2 -1/2 pounds)

A fresh beef tongue (2 −2 -1/2 pounds) or 2 veal tongues

2 pounds oxtail, cut into 1 -inch-thick disks

4 −5 pounds soup bones, cut into walnut-sized pieces (not larger!)

1 tablespoon shortening

5 or 6 kinds of soup vegetables (4 −5 carrots, 2 −3 parsley roots, 2 −3 white turnips, 1 large yellow turnip, 2 −3 kohlrabi, 1/2 to 1/4 small head of cabbage)

2 lemon-sized onions, unpeeled, one studded with 2 −3 whole cloves

1 leek

4 −5 small shallots, skin on

2 −3 large cloves of garlic

1 bunch flat-leaf parsley

12 black peppercorns and 12 white peppercorns, both slightly bruised

1 bay leaf

2 −3 tablespoons Chef's Salt per quart water

In a large, heavy frying pan, place 1 tablespoon shortening (anything but margarine), brown the cut-up bones, sprinkled with a little salt, over high heat until the bones start to turn dark brown. Add the bones to the roasting pan. Cut one of the onions in half, including the skin, and add a few cloves of garlic, half of the peppercorns, bay leaf. Add the peelings and trimmings of all the vegetables you use but not the vegetables. Add the spices. Pour 1 quart water on all this and place it in the oven at 300 degrees. Increase the heat to 450 degrees after 30 minutes. Turn the bones frequently for the next 10 minutes, then remove the roasting pan from the oven and reserve the bones, onion, garlic, and spices.

Strain the liquid in which the bones have roasted and return to the roasting pan. Rub the meats (brisket, shank, and oxtail) with

2–3 tablespoons Chef's Salt and add to the pan. Add the peeled, cleaned vegetables. Fill the pan with water, add more Chef's Salt, the rest of the pepper, bay leaf, etc. Cover the roasting pan and put it in the oven for 2-1/2 to 3 hours at 300 degrees and go on with the preparation of the rest of the meal.

Make the creamed spinach, the other vegetable dish of your choice, the pan-roasted potatoes, and the apple horseradish.

When the beef has been in the oven for 1 hour, add the beef tongue and continue cooking. If the tongue was veal rather than beef tongue, add it 1-1/2 hours into the cooking process.

When the meat has been in the oven for 3 hours, remove it from the pan, strain the liquid, and prepare a board which will be used for slicing the meats. Pour the liquid into a tall, narrow vessel suitable for skimming off the fat, pile the soup vegetables onto a serving platter together with the oxtail disks, and cover with aluminum foil. The meat will be firm but easy to cut with a good knife. If you don't have the divided platters used to serve this dish in Austria, use your largest dining plates, prewarmed. Place the vegetables in bowls.

When the vegetable dishes are already on the table, slice the meats, definitely against the grain, approximately 1/4 inch to 1/2 inch thick, and arrange them on a large platter, or arrange one slice of each kind of meat on each plate and let the guests around the table help themselves to the other dishes. Bring the wonderful broth the meat was prepared in to the table in a gravy boat as well as the platter of soup vegetables. Now the joy of the Tafelspitz is ready to begin! Serves 8–10.

POTAGE CAMÉRANI

This is a very old recipe for a dish which is really an entrée rather than a soup.

Vegetables
Macaroni
Boiled chicken
12 chicken livers (optional)
Parmesan cheese

Butter
Bread crumbs
Bouillon

Sauté a cup of julienned vegetables in butter, and if you like, add 12 chicken livers cut in very small dice. Cook 1/4 pound macaroni in salted water, drain, dress with butter, and season. In a serving dish lined with butter and bread crumbs, alternate layers of macaroni, poultry meat, and the chicken liver mixture, sprinkling each layer with grated Parmesan. Moisten with bouillon and bake.

ROAST VEAL

1 5- to 6-pound leg of veal, boned, rolled, and tied
3 tablespoons Chef's Salt
2 tablespoons butter
2 tablespoons oil
Paprika
2 medium-sized onions, sliced
1 medium-sized carrot, sliced
2 stalks celery, chopped
1 clove garlic, crushed
4 to 6 cups veal or chicken stock
1 bay leaf
1 teaspoon crushed thyme
1 cup light cream
1 cup dry white wine
2 teaspoons cornstarch
2 tablespoons water

Preheat oven to 350 degrees. Rub the roast with 2 tablespoons oil, then with the crushed garlic and Chef's Salt. Spread surface with softened butter and sprinkle with paprika.

Place the onions, carrots, and celery in the bottom of a roasting pan. Place the roast on top.

Add bay leaf, thyme, and enough stock to cover the vegetables.

Cover with lid or with double layer of aluminum foil and place in oven. Cook for approximately 1 hour. Remove cover. Continue to cook uncovered until a meat thermometer registers 160 degrees when inserted in the thickest part of the roast.

Remove from oven, untie roast, and place it on a carving platter. Keep warm.

Remove vegetables from the pan, discard bay leaf, and place the vegetables in a blender with a little of the skimmed pan juices. Blend into a fine puree.

Place puree in a saucepan with the strained, skimmed pan juices. Slowly add light cream and wine and bring to a boil, stirring constantly.

Dissolve the cornstarch in the water and stir into the sauce. Whip over low heat until sauce is thick and smooth. Season with additional salt if necessary. Strain through a sieve into a sauceboat. Serve hot with the carved veal.

The butter spread on the roast will give an exceptionally good flavor and, with the paprika sprinkled over the top, a nice brown color. Rubbing the veal with oil first prevents evaporation of inside juices during cooking and helps the spices to adhere to the surface.

Be sure to let the roast stand at least 30 minutes in a warm place, covered, before attempting to slice. Otherwise, it will fall apart.

FILLET À LA TRAUTTMANSDORFF
Beef tenderloin
Chicken risotto

Roast a beef tenderloin just until rare. Arrange slices of meat around an oval platter and mound chicken risotto in the center. If individual servings are desired, place risotto on each plate with a slice of meat on either side. Pour juice from the roast over the dish.

ROAST TENDERLOIN
5 to 6 pounds untrimmed or 3 to 3-1/2 pounds
trimmed tenderloin
1 tablespoon Chef's Salt
1 teaspoon coarse black pepper or 1/2 teaspoon fine black pepper

1/2 teaspoon sugar

2 to 3 tablespoons Kitchen Bouquet

1/2 cup corn oil

1 cup lard, bacon drippings, or oil

1 cup red wine or canned consommé

2 envelopes Knox gelatin (2 tablespoons)

Rub the whole surface of the tenderloin with the sugar, salt, pepper. Mix the Kitchen Bouquet with the 1/2 cup corn oil, pour the mixture onto the beef, and massage it in. Let it stand at room temperature.

Preheat the broiler. Line the broiling pan with aluminum foil. Place the tenderloin on it and bring it as close to the source of heat as possible. Turn it every 2 to 3 minutes until the whole surface is seared. Let the tenderloin cool at room temperature. Sprinkle with 2 envelopes Knox gelatin, rub it in the surface.

Wrap the tenderloin in heavy-duty aluminum foil, pouring the wine (or consommé) over the meat before closing the foil on top.

Preheat the oven to 450 degrees. Roast the foil-wrapped tenderloin at 450 degrees for 20 minutes for rare, 25–30 minutes for medium-rare. Remove. Let it cool at room temperature. This can be done in the morning and the meat can stay at room temperature all day long (except on hot summer days, when you would refrigerate it if it were to stand longer than 2 hours at room temperature).

Half an hour before serving, heat the 1 cup of shortening in a small saucepan until it reaches the smoking point. Place the tenderloin on a cookie sheet covered with aluminum foil. Pour the smoking hot fat over the surface of the meat and roast, uncovered, at 450 to 500 degrees for 10 to 15 minutes. Let it sit for 10 minutes before slicing.

CHICKEN RISOTTO

2 cups rice

1 package frozen green peas

8 ounces chicken livers

4 tablespoons oil
1 small clove garlic
Béchamel sauce
2 tablespoons butter
Black pepper and salt to taste
1 cup grated Romano, Parmesan, or similar hard cheese

Cook the rice in lightly salted water according to package directions. Do not overcook. Quickly rinse the rice in a colander under running cold water. Shake as dry as possible.

Prepare a béchamel sauce.

While the rice cooks, heat the 4 tablespoons oil with the garlic, slightly crushed, until the edges of the garlic start to brown. Remove and discard the garlic clove.

Pat the chicken livers dry with a paper towel. Grind fresh pepper over each chicken liver but do not salt them.

Fry the livers in a covered frying pan over medium heat, being sure they do not touch each other and turning once in a while. To test for doneness, pierce the thickest part of a liver with a knife point or a fork. If no more red liquid comes out, they are done. Remove them from the fire and keep covered in a warm place.

Cook green peas according to package directions.

To serve, slice as many nice, even slices as possible from the larger parts of the chicken livers. Salt the remaining pieces and mince them so they are about the size of the peas. Gently mix together the rice, béchamel sauce, green peas, and minced chicken livers.

Press the mixture into a bowl which has been brushed with the 2 tablespoons butter. Unmold the rice on a serving platter. Arrange the slices of chicken liver around the edge of the rice and sprinkle all the cheese on the top.

Note: It is important that you do not salt the chicken livers before cooking, as salting will make them tough. If the frying is done over high heat, the edges will be tough and brittle. If done over low heat, they will become soft and unpleasant. This is why it is so important to maintain a medium heat.

Patting the livers dry also helps to insure the proper texture. Covering the pan saves your hands because chicken livers tend to spatter while frying.

HUNGARIAN GOULASH OR PAPRIKASH

2 pounds beef chuck, cut into 1-inch cubes
Chef's Salt
Freshly ground black pepper to taste
1/2 cup lard or chicken fat
2-1/2 to 3 cups onions, peeled and finely chopped
2 tablespoons sweet Hungarian paprika
2 tablespoons flour
3 cups water or beef stock
2 tablespoons tomato paste
1 teaspoon caraway seeds, slightly bruised
2 cups sour cream (if served as paprikash)

Season meat with Chef's Salt and additional black pepper. In a large, heavy saucepan, heat the lard or oil to the smoking point. Brown the meat in the lard, turning with a spatula so that it browns on all sides. Add onions and cook until they become limp. Sprinkle the paprika and flour over the meat and onions. Cook for 2 minutes on low heat, stirring to keep the mixture from sticking.

Add the water or beef stock, tomato paste, and caraway seeds. Stir. Simmer, covered, over low heat for 1-1/2 hours or until meat is tender. Check occasionally to see if there is enough liquid; if necessary, add more.

Serve from a large casserole. If the dish is served as paprikash, serve it with the sour cream on the side in a sauceboat.

If possible, use imported Hungarian or Spanish paprika; they will give the real flavor. But if you can't get either, add 1/4 teaspoon sugar to the paprika you are using.

If you double this recipe, by all means buy a piece of shank, with the marrow bone in it if possible, and add this to the meat for the goulash. It will greatly improve the taste. Some of the goulash may be frozen for later use.

GOULASH À LA DEBRECEN

Beef goulash
Soup greens, diced fine
Small pickles, cut lengthwise (tiny dill or Kosher style)

Cook a good beef goulash. When it is partly braised, add diced soup greens. To serve, garnish with small dill pickles sliced lengthwise.

GOULASH SUPREME

Beef goulash
1 part pork
1 part veal
Flour
Stock

Braise beef goulash until partly done. Then add one part pork, one part veal. When done, dust the goulash with flour and dilute with stock to finish the sauce.

SZÉKELY GOULASH

5 tablespoons shortening (rendered from the trimmings if you like)
2 pounds pork butt, trimmed and cut into 1-inch cubes
1/3 cup flour
1 tablespoon Chef's Salt
1 clove garlic, mashed with 1/2 teaspoon Chef's Salt
1 cup finely minced onion
2/3 cup tomato juice
1/2 cup chopped green pepper
2 tablespoons Hungarian paprika
2 to 2-1/2 pounds sauerkraut, drained and rinsed
1/2 teaspoon caraway seed, bruised
1/4 teaspoon white peppercorns, bruised
1 bay leaf
1/2 cup grated raw potato
1 pound Hungarian, Polish, or similar smoked sausage or ring bologna
1 cup sour cream
1 cup buttermilk

Heat 4 tablespoons shortening in a large skillet. Dredge the pork cubes in a mixture of flour, Chef's Salt, and garlic. Place in a skillet with 2/3 cup minced onion and cook over low heat 20 minutes, stirring occasionally, until the meat browns.

Add tomato juice, green pepper, and paprika. Cover and simmer over low heat 1-1/4 to 1-1/2 hours, until the meat is tender. Add water as necessary to keep the meat barely covered and stir occasionally to prevent the meat from sticking to the pan. Remove from heat and set aside.

In the remaining 1 tablespoon shortening, sauté the remaining 1/3 cup onion until golden. Press the sauerkraut, reserving the juice, and rinse under cold running water. Press dry again by handfuls to remove all liquid and discard this liquid. Loosen the sauerkraut with your fingers and add to the onions. Add caraway seed, white peppercorns, bay leaf, and water to cover. Bring to a boil over medium heat, then reduce heat and simmer 2-1/2 hours. Grate the potato into the simmering sauerkraut and stir in gently. Taste and correct seasoning by adding some of the reserved sauerkraut juice if the taste is too bland.

To serve, gently mix pork goulash with cooked sauerkraut. Slice the sausage thin and stir it in until it warms through. Add some of the hot liquid to sour cream and buttermilk in a bowl. Stir, then add mixture to the goulash (in this way you avoid curdling the sour cream). Serve with plain boiled potatoes.

Instead of slicing the sausage into the goulash, you may sauté the sausage pieces in a very little shortening over medium heat and use them to decorate the serving dish. You may also replace part of the sour cream, if you wish, with yogurt.

POULTRY RICE WITH PARMESAN
4 cups steamed rice (2 cups uncooked)
1-1/2 pounds poultry, cooked (one 3-pound chicken, whole)
1 each giblets, liver (from one chicken)
1/4 cup lemon juice
1 pinch nutmeg
2 cups white sauce

2 *teaspoons butter*

2/3 *cup Parmesan cheese, grated*

Steam rice, then cook poultry, including giblets. Sauté liver in a little butter. Cut the meat, giblets, and liver into small pieces, season with a bit of lemon juice and nutmeg. Prepare a béchamel sauce using the soup in which the poultry was boiled and add it to the meat. Butter a mold, put into it a layer of rice, then a layer of meat, then another layer of rice. Turn out onto a serving dish and top with Parmesan. In place of Parmesan, finely chopped ham can be used. In that case the dish is called Rice à la Turque.

HUNGARIAN STUFFED CABBAGE

1 head cabbage (approximately 2-1/2 –3 pounds)

1-1/2 pounds finely ground lean pork

1 cup sautéed onion

2 tablespoons parsley (finely chopped)

1 tablespoon salt

1 large egg plus 2 tablespoons water

1/4 teaspoon white pepper

2 cups steamed rice

2 pounds sauerkraut

1 pint sour cream

2/3 tablespoon paprika

1 cup (or more) bread crumbs

6 –8 strips breakfast bacon

Remove the outside green leaves and the core from a head of cabbage. In a pot with the lid on, blanch the cabbage by sub-merging it in enough lightly salted water to cover. Mix the ground pork, lightly sautéed onion and parsley, the egg, and steamed rice. Season with salt, 1/3 tablespoon paprika, and white pepper. Cut the ribs out of 16 blanched cabbage leaves. Divide the pork mixture into 16 portions by laying it on a flat surface, patting it into a flat and square piece, and making 3 hor-izontal then 3 vertical cuts to obtain 16 pieces. Fill the leaves with the meat mixture. Roll them up but not too tightly. Cut the rest of the head cabbage fine, squeeze out the sauerkraut, then mix the two and cook. Thicken the sauerkraut slightly with a large raw potato grated into it while cooling, then place half of it in a layer about a finger thick into the bottom of a roasting pan. Add the cabbage rolls, the second layer of the sauerkraut, a bit of sour cream, the rest of the paprika and sprinkle with the bread crumbs, cover with the 6 strips of bacon, and bake at 325 degrees for about 30–35 minutes or until golden brown.

JELLIED GOOSE

1 meaty goose
4 tablespoons shortening
Garlic
1 tablespoon Chef's Salt
Pepper
Bay leaf
Salt
Allspice
Egg white
Carrots
Celery
Large onion

Veal Aspic
2 veal shanks
Flavored vinegar

Gelatin Aspic
8–10 envelopes of unflavored Knox gelatin
4 tablespoons water
Flavored vinegar

Ask your butcher to quarter a goose with a poultry saw. Reserve the giblets. Remove the large lumps of fat under the skin and cut them into small pieces, add the 4 tablespoons shortening, and render out the goose fat in a small, heavy pot over medium heat. Mash the garlic with 1 tablespoon of Chef's Salt. Rub all surfaces of the goose with this mixture and place the pieces on a low-edged pan. Strain the rendered goose fat and then heat it to the smoking point. Pour half of it over the breast of the goose, then turn the goose breast-side down and pour the other half of the hot fat over it. Add water to a roasting pan to a depth of 2 inches, dissolve the remaining Chef's Salt in it, then place the goose into the pan. Add 2 large carrots, 4 ribs of celery, 2 large onions with skin, all coarsely chopped, 2 large cloves of garlic, bay leaf, allspice, and 1/2 teaspoon slightly bruised black pepper. At this point, decide whether to use a veal aspic or a gelatin aspic.

Veal Aspic: If you want to be 100 percent authentic, ask your butcher for 2 veal knuckles, each cut into 4 pieces. Cooking the veal together with the goose will yield a gelatinlike substance for the aspic. Cover the roasting pan and roast at 300 degrees for approximately 3 hours or until a thermometer inserted into the thickest part of the thigh and into the breast registers 180 degrees. At this point, remove the roasting pan from the oven and let it stand, covered, for about 30 minutes. Then remove the pieces of meat and allow to cool on a tray until they can be touched. With a sharp paring knife or small butcher knife, remove the breast and thigh meat from bones, keeping the pieces of meat as large as possible. Pour the juices from the roasting pan into a fairly tall, narrow container to allow the fat to come to the top. Skim off as much as possible. Refrigerate the roasting liquid until all the fat can be removed. This liquid will be the aspic. Clarify the chilled, defatted liquid by adding one beaten egg white for each quart of stock. Stir, bring to a boil, and simmer until the liquid clears. Strain through a colander lined with a damp cloth. If you wish, flavor it with a good balsamic vinegar, tarragon vinegar, or flavored vinegar of choice. If you wish, use plain Japanese rice wine vinegar or rice vinegar and for each 2 tablespoons of vinegar, add 1 teaspoon sugar.

Gelatin Aspic: If you are more interested in results than method, you did not use the veal knuckles. Dissolve 8 envelopes of unflavored Knox gelatin in approximately 4 tablespoons of water. Strain cooking liquid through a fine sieve lined with a damp cloth and add the gelatin. You must have a total of 3 quarts liquid. If there is less, add water. Adjust salt and add a few drops of yellow liquid food color. You may flavor the aspic with a good balsamic vinegar, tarragon vinegar, or flavored vinegar of choice. This will be the aspic into which you place the portions of goose.

At this point, you have two choices: you can either put all the meat, sliced, into one elegant container or arrange it in individual dishes. If you make 8–12 portions of jellied goose you will have plenty of scraps for other purposes, like potted ground goose (see recipe below).

Slice de-boned thighs and breasts diagonally against the grain. Top each arrangement with overlapping slices of breast meat. Cover with the aspic.

To set the aspic, place in a cold room for 4 or 5 hours or in the refrigerator for 2 or 3 hours. If you are a beginner, it is perhaps advisable to test the aspic by placing a saucer of the gelatinous liquid (2 to 3 tablespoons) near the bottom of the freezer. If it is still liquid after 15 minutes, add a couple of envelopes of gelatin to either kind of aspic.

Potted Ground Goose: Combine all the goose skin and the remaining meat with cooked giblets and grind once through the medium blade of a meat grinder, season the mixture to taste with black pepper, minced garlic or salt, and 1 or 2 herbs of your choice (tarragon, rosemary, flat parsley, shallots) which have been lightly sautéed in a small amount of goose fat. Press the mixture into a small container so that it is close to full. Keep for up to a week in a refrigerator or 2–4 months in a freezer. Unmold to serve and decorate with sliced cooked carrot, small mushroom caps, or pitted prunes.

STUFFED POTATOES

6–8 large potatoes
Shellfish (1/2 pound cooked, cleaned lobster meat plus 1 pound
cooked, peeled, and deveined shrimp or 1-1/2 pounds lobster for 6,
2 pounds for 8, figuring 4 ounces cooked shellfish for 8)
6–8 eggs poached for 3 minutes or soft-boiled and peeled
6–8 thin slices of truffles
Shellfish sauce

On a baking sheet, bake very large potatoes in the oven. Scoop out the potatoes but leave a wall and keep a cover attached so as to form a box. Before serving, stuff the potatoes with shellfish in shellfish sauce, top with a peeled 3-minute egg. Wedge the potato cover open with a slice of truffle.

SHELLFISH SAUCE
2 tablespoons corn oil
2 tablespoons finely chopped shallots or scallions, white parts only
1 cup water
2 tablespoons cornstarch
1 tablespoon Hungarian mild paprika
1 cup light cream
1/2 cup sherry
Pinch sugar
1 teaspoon Chef's Salt
2 tablespoons butter at room temperature
4 ounces lightly prepoached lobster or shrimp meat

In a sauté pan, heat the corn oil. Add the shallots and sauté 5 minutes or until they start to get limp and yellow. Add 2 to 3 tablespoons water and stir until it evaporates. Add more water and repeat until you notice that the shallots disappear and the mixture turns into an opaque pulp.

Mix the cornstarch and paprika into the light cream and with a wire whip stir this mixture into the shallot mixture. Add sherry, sugar, and Chef's Salt, and keep stirring. Add about 1/2 cup more water, if needed, for an even, smooth, medium-thick sauce. Lower the heat and simmer, stirring occasionally, for 10 minutes. Add the soft butter in small pieces, beating after each addition to the sauce. With a cooking spoon, fold in the chopped poached lobster or shrimp. Simmer 2 to 3 minutes, then remove from heat, cover, and let the sauce steep for at least 10 minutes before serving. Correct seasoning.

OMELETTE

Among the several things you cannot learn from books are ice skating and omelette making. Still, in case you don't have your own excellent recipe for a 2-egg omelette, try this one. Beat 2 fresh medium or large eggs with 3 tablespoons milk, a pinch of salt, a pinch of ground white pepper. Preheat a standard 6-inch omelette pan, which you never use for any other purpose, over slow heat. When the pan is well prewarmed, add 1 tablespoon oil and 1/2 tablespoon butter, swirl butter around in pan by tilting it back and forward, left and right, until shortening coats the whole surface. Beat egg mixture again, pour quickly into pan, and stir immediately with a rubber spatula. Place filling about one-third of the way from the far end and immediately start to fold while the egg mixture is still running over and around filling, with the first fold covering the filling. Flip omelette onto a dinner plate, covering the already folded two-thirds with the remaining one-third. In Katharina Schratt's day, omelettes were usually made with separately whipped whites. This made them lighter and fluffier.

OMELETTE À LA GUTENBERG
Goose liver puree
The omelette is filled with goose liver puree.

OMELETTE À LA PORTUGAISE
Tomato
Butter
Garnish a plain omelette with pieces of tomato sautéed in butter.

OMELETTE À LA PROVENÇALE
Tomato
Sliced sausages
The same as Omelette à la portugaise, but add slices of fried French or cippolata-style sausage.

OMELETTE WITH LOBSTER
Lobster pieces
Butter
The omelette is filled with lobster pieces sautéed in butter.

OMELETTE À LA REINE
Chicken puree
The omelette is filled with chicken puree.

EGGS À LA REINE
Poached eggs
Toast
Chicken puree
Truffles
Spread toast rounds with chicken puree, top with poached eggs on toast, and finish with truffles.

EGGS À L'IMPERIALE
Poached eggs
Goose liver puree
Madeira sauce
Toast
Spread toast rounds with goose liver puree, top with poached eggs, and finish with madeira sauce.

For this recipe, you may use a good brand of canned natural goose liver or pâté or, if you wish, your own prepared goose liver. For each portion, add 1 tablespoon goose liver in any form or pâté and 1 teaspoon butter at room temperature to a blender with a few grains of salt and a pinch of pâté spice, a drop of essence of truffle, or a drop or two of brandy or cognac. Work until smooth, chill slightly before using.

EGGS À L'AMÉRICAINE
Poached eggs
Ham
Toast, either cut round or oval with a cookie cutter or cut into triangles
Tomato sauce

Place ham on toast, top with poached egg, and finish with a tomato sauce.

For the tomato sauce, take for each egg 3 tablespoons undiluted Campbell's tomato soup, 1 tablespoon ketchup, and 1/4 teaspoon sugar or brown sugar, or any of the good brands of canned tomato sauce. If you wish, you may season the sauce with a dash of Tabasco, Worcestershire sauce, a drop of lemon, or a spoonful of red vermouth, sherry, or brandy.

DESSERTS AND PASTRIES

YEAST DOUGH RAISIN CAKE

1 package active dry yeast
1/4 cup warm water
1/2 cup milk
1/4 cup soft butter
1 tablespoon sugar
3/4 teaspoon salt

2 large eggs
2 cups sifted flour
Extra melted butter for brushing
Raisins

Dissolve the yeast in warm water. Scald the milk. Stir in the butter, sugar, and salt. Cool to lukewarm. Combine the eggs with the yeast and the milk. Add the flour. Beat the dough vigorously until smooth. Cover and let rise in a warm, draft-free place for about 1 hour or until it doubles in size. Preheat the oven to 375 degrees. Stir the dough well. Spoon it into greased muffin pans, filling each about half full. Let rise again in a warm place until double in size. Brush the dough with beaten egg whites, sprinkle with sugar and raisins, and brush with a bit of melted butter. Bake.

Be sure that you do not mix the yeast and egg into the milk before it cools to lukewarm. If the milk is too hot, it will impair the yeast's ability to rise and may partially cook the eggs.

BASTA FLORA CAKE

5 ounces flour
5 ounces butter, very cold
2-1/2 ounces sugar
4–6 ounces baking chocolate, grated
3 yolks
Cloves
Cinnamon
Currant preserve

Preheat the oven to 375 degrees. Sift the flour into the middle of a pastry board or onto a clean kitchen table so that it looks like a wide-based cone.

Make a well in the middle and add the sugar, the grated chocolate, eggs, and spices. Dust the surface of the cold butter with flour and start breaking the butter into small pieces, dipping your fingers into the flour before breaking each piece. Continue until all the pieces of butter are about the size of an almond or smaller.

Quickly mix the dough together with your fingertips, incorporating the flour from the outside into the middle. If the dough should be too soft to roll out, pat it into the bottom of a cake pan. Reserve about one-third of the dough and form a lattice to cover the cake. Bake at 375 degrees for 15 minutes, lower the temperature to 325 degrees and bake for 15 minutes more. When the cake is done, fill the lattice with the currant preserve.

SNOWBALLS

2-1/2 cups flour

1-3/4 cups butter

1 cup sugar

1 large egg

1/2 teaspoon baking powder

Grated zest of 1/2 lemon

Sift the flour into the middle of a pastry board or onto a clean, even-surfaced kitchen table so that the flour looks like a wide-based cone.

Make a well in the middle and add the sugar, baking powder, egg, and grated lemon rind. Dust the surface of the butter with flour and start breaking the butter into small pieces, dipping your fingers into the flour before breaking each piece. Continue until all the pieces of butter are about the size of an almond or smaller.

Quickly mix the dough together with your fingertips, incorporating the flour from the outside into the middle. Roll out the dough and, with a cookie cutter, cut out rounds about 2-1/2 inches across. With a pastry wheel, cut four parallel slits through the rounds without cutting into the border. This will form three strips attached to the border. Fry in deep fat. Dust with powdered sugar.

Note: The zest is the outermost yellow layer of the skin, without the white pulp. The best way to remove it is to use a lemon-zester. This is a small, triangular-shaped metal tool mounted on a wooden or plastic handle. The tip of the triangle is attached to the handle; the base has a row of four or five holes, which take off the zest perfectly. If you do not have this tool or cannot obtain it in a shop, you can use a grater—very carefully so as not to grate the white bitter pulp along with the skin.

VANILLA CRESCENTS

3 cups flour
8 ounces ground almonds (approximately 2-1/2 cups)
1 cup powdered sugar
1 cup unsalted butter
2 egg yolks
2 cups or more powdered sugar kept in a screw-top jar with
vanilla beans for a week or longer for dusting cookies

In a bowl, combine flour, almonds, and powdered sugar. Blend in butter as you would for pie pastry. Beat egg yolks with a fork and slowly work them into the mixture. Don't overwork. Let the dough rest in the refrigerator at least 30 minutes. Preheat oven to 325 degrees. Form small crescents and bake until they dry out, about 15 minutes. Remove cookies from cookie sheet and sprinkle very generously with vanilla sugar while hot.

This is a very fine cookie—a bit time consuming, especially the first time you make it, but very rewarding.

The best way to form the crescents is to divide the dough into four equal parts and then pat out each part with a light hand into strips approximately 2 inches wide by 6 inches long. Divide the strip in half, then each half into half, continuing until you have approximately 12 to 14 small strips about 1/2 inch wide and 1-1/2 to 2 inches long. Gently bend the strips one by one into crescent shapes right on cookie sheet.

In many specialty stores you can buy vanilla beans (5 to 6 inches long, 1/4 inch thick). Keep them in a tight-fitting screw-top jar filled with powdered sugar. Fresh beans are moist, pliable, and fragrant; old ones are dry, dark gray, and brittle. Buy the fresh ones!

Makes approximately 4 dozen cookies. Store the cookies in a metal cookie box with a waxed paper liner between each layer of cookies. They will keep for 3 to 4 weeks in a cool place.

STICKS À LA PALFFY

4 ounces flour
2 ounces butter
1 ounce sugar

Salt

3 tablespoons milk

Egg wash for brushing

1 small egg

1 tablespoon cold water

Quickly work the ingredients into a dough, being careful to handle the butter as described in other short-dough recipes so that it does not melt. Let the dough rest for a bit.

Roll out the dough and, using a pastry wheel, form little sticks as thin as knitting needles. Place them on a lightly buttered baking sheet and brush them with egg wash made with 1 egg and 1 tablespoon cold water. Bake them in a moderate oven (350 degrees) until they are golden brown. When cool, arrange them on a serving plate in a lattice.

YEAST PRETZEL

1 recipe as for Yeast Dough Raisin Cake (see page 175).

Butter prepared as below, 1/4 pound for each pound dough

Raisins

Lemon glaze

This is a delicate, flaky dough, similar to the one used for croissants or the very best "Danish" pastry. You may try it a few times before you master it, but it is well worth the effort, and the dough can be adapted to many different uses.

Mix a dough as for Yeast Dough Raisin Cake. After letting it rise in a warm place for an hour, beat it down, then weigh it and let it rest in the refrigerator for about 20 minutes.

In the meantime, prepare the butter. For each pound of dough, use 1/4 pound butter. It must be flexible enough to roll into the dough but cool enough so that it never disappears. The delicious flakiness results from having little bits of unmelted butter dotted throughout the dough as it goes into the oven. The best butter for this purpose is unsalted butter, because of its characteristic texture. You may either beat the butter until it is creamy and return it briefly to the refrigerator or knead it under cold running water until it is elastic and then pat dry.

Remove the dough from the refrigerator and roll it into a

rectangle about 3/8 inch thick. Dot one-third of the butter over the surface of the dough in small bits. Fold the dough into thirds like a letter and turn the dough by one quarter turn. Roll it lightly into an oblong 3/8 inch thick and repeat the process twice more, until all the butter has been used. During the third rolling add raisins to the dough. Remember to work swiftly and lightly. Let the dough rest in the refrigerator for 20 minutes.

Make long, thin rolls of dough and form them into pretzels, let them rise until almost double in bulk, and bake them at 375 degrees for about 15 minutes. Ice the cooled pretzels with lemon glaze.

LEMON GLAZE

Mix juice and grated lemon rind of 1 lemon to 1 cup of sifted confectioners' sugar. Mix well and brush onto the pretzels with a soft pastry brush.

PISTACHIO CREAM

8 ounces very finely ground pistachios
16–20 blanched almonds, finely ground
8 tablespoons sugar
A few grains salt
1 pint whipping cream
1 envelope unflavored gelatin
2 tablespoons cold water
6 tablespoons boiling water

Dissolve the gelatin in 2 tablespoons cold water, add 6 tablespoons boiling water, boil over medium heat for 1 minute, then remove from heat and cool until it reaches the consistency of Karo syrup.

Grind pistachios and almonds fine, preferably in a European-style nut grinder.

Whip the cream very stiff with a few grains of salt and 3 tablespoons sugar. Fold the cream into the ground nuts and remaining sugar alternately with the gelatin mixture, poured in a thin stream.

Divide the cream among eight dessert glasses and refrigerate. Allow to stand at room temperature briefly before serving.

SALT STICKS

1 cup (2 sticks) salted butter
3 egg yolks
6 cups flour
1/2 package dry yeast
5 tablespoons warm milk
Dash of sugar
Dash of salt
1/3 cup warm water
1 egg
3 teaspoons caraway seeds
1/2 cup coarse salt (Kosher salt)

Mix the butter and egg yolks in an electric mixer equipped with a paddle or dough hook. Slowly incorporate all but a few tablespoons of the flour. Dissolve the yeast in the warm milk. Add the yeast mixture to the flour mixture along with the sugar, salt, and water.

Keep mixing until the dough no longer sticks to the sides of the bowl. The dough will be somewhat crumbly, not very moist. Roll the dough out on a floured board to approximately 1/4 inch thick. With a pastry wheel, cut pieces 1/3 by 3 inches.

By hand, shape both ends of each piece of dough to form a point. Place the pieces on a lightly greased baking sheet. Cover with a towel and let them rest in a warm place 15 to 20 minutes. Preheat the oven to 350 degrees to 375 degrees. Beat the egg, then run it through a sieve. Brush the top of each salt stick with egg and sprinkle generously with coarse salt and caraway seeds. Bake the salt sticks for approximately 12 minutes or until the points are browned.

It is hard to give an exact baking time or temperature for this simple recipe. Only your own experience will teach you how hot an oven you should have, or how long you should bake, or how long you should mix the dough before rolling it out. But if you master this dough, you will be very proud of it.

These salt sticks are versatile — they can be served with scrambled eggs for breakfast, with soup and salad at lunch, as an appetizer, or with cheese for dessert.

If you cannot get coarse or Kosher salt, mix regular table salt with a little water so that it gets very thick, like a syrup. Dribble some of the mixture over the salt sticks after they have baked for 2 to 3 minutes. They will have little white salt dribblings resembling small pieces of popcorn, as sometimes seen on a professional baker's salt sticks.

NAPOLEON CAKES

4 ounces sugar

3 eggs

2 yolks

2 ounces flour

1/3 cup almonds, finely slivered

1 tablespoon sugar

Apricot jam

Beat sugar, eggs, and yolks in an electric mixer until they turn pale yellow and thick. Sift the flour over the egg mixture and fold in with a rubber spatula. Roast finely slivered almonds in sugar for a few minutes at 300 degrees and fold into the batter. Spread the batter on a buttered and generously floured baking sheet not larger than 8 inches by 12 inches. Bake at 375 degrees for just a few minutes, lower the temperature to 250 degrees and bake for another couple of minutes. When it is cool, cut the cake into serving-size slices and put two slices together with apricot jam between them.

GENUINE PISCHINGER GÂTEAU

5 ounces sugar

2 handfuls peeled hazelnuts, ground (approximately 1 cup)

Vanilla from vanilla bean (split a 1-1/2 inch to 2 inch length of vanilla bean, scrape pulp and seeds, discard skin or place it back into the jar with the powdered sugar)

6 eggs

9 ounces butter
3 ounces sugar
10 ounces softened chocolate
Karlsbad wafers
Chocolate glaze, purchased or prepared according to
directions on chocolate package

Put in a large bowl 5 ounces sugar and 2 handfuls peeled hazel-nuts, ground; scrape in some vanilla seeds from a split vanilla bean, and add 6 eggs. Mix well and stir over boiling water until thick. Let the egg cream cool. Cream 9 ounces butter, 3 ounces sugar, 10 ounces softened chocolate and add the egg cream, one tablespoon at a time. Spread this filling between Karlsbad wafers, making seven layers, and cover the cake with a chocolate glaze. Karlsbad wafers are available in different sizes, so this recipe can be prepared either as individual cakes or one large one.

PARFAIT FÜRST PÜCKLER

For the First Mixture
1 pint heavy cream
Pinch salt
2 eggs, separated
Vanilla (preferably from bean)
4 teaspoons sugar
4 tablespoons powdered sugar

For the Second Mixture
1 pint heavy cream
8 tablespoons sugar
4 tablespoons cocoa
1 egg
2 tablespoons brandy
Pinch salt

For the Third Mixture
1 pint heavy cream
1 envelope unflavored gelatin

3 tablespoons water

1/2 cup water

1 cup puree of fresh strawberries

6 tablespoons sugar

Pinch salt

Line a three-quart oblong container with aluminum foil as follows: First place in the bottom a strip as wide as the bottom but long enough to come up the two ends with 4 additional inches of foil on each end. Then line the dish with another piece of foil covering the width and coming up the two sides with 4 additional inches on each side.

Prepare the first mixture by beating the heavy cream with the salt and the sugar until it forms stiff peaks. Lightly beat the egg yolks with the vanilla and gently stir this mixture into the whipped cream. Beat the egg whites with the powdered sugar until they are stiff but not dry. Gently fold the cream–egg yolk mixture into the foil-lined dish and place it in the freezer until firm.

Prepare the second mixture by beating the heavy cream until it is stiff, adding the sugar gradually. Beat the egg with the cocoa, brandy, and salt until mixture is frothy. Gently fold the egg-cocoa-brandy mixture into the heavy cream. Pour over the first mixture and place in the freezer again until firm.

Prepare the strawberry puree by first cutting the strawberries in small pieces while holding them in your hand, then gently pressing them with a silver or stainless steel fork in a sieve and collecting the liquid as it runs off. Add the sugar to the liquid. Dissolve the gelatin in the 3 tablespoons of water. Bring the 1/2 cup water to a boil and add the dissolved gelatin. Cool in an ice-water bath. Beat the heavy cream until stiff, adding the salt. Pour the gelatin over the surface of the cream and gently fold it in. Add the strawberry puree, folding all ingredients together. Pour this mixture over the top of the chocolate mixture. Place in the freezer. As soon as the top mixture is firm, fold the aluminum foil from all four sides over the parfait and keep it frozen.

To serve, cut very thin slices from the parfait with a hot, wet knife.

The original of this ice cream recipe was named after a German prince who was a great gourmet. It is the finest ice cream dish imaginable, but do not serve too much because it is so rich. As you can see, besides the flavorings, only one ingredient — whipped cream — is used.

NUT ROLL

For the Cake
6 eggs
6 heaping tablespoons sugar
6 tablespoons finely ground walnuts
1 tablespoon fine white fresh bread crumbs (see appendix)
1/4 teaspoon baking powder

For the Icing
1 cup unsalted butter
1 egg
8 to 10 tablespoons powdered sugar
8 to 10 tablespoons Dutch cocoa
1 tablespoon boiling water
1 to 2 tablespoons brandy or rum (optional)

Preheat oven to 375 degrees. Grind the nuts. Beat eggs with sugar in an electric mixer at high speed for 15 to 20 minutes or until they are lemon-colored, light, and fluffy like whipped cream just before it starts to form peaks. By hand, gently fold in the ground nuts (sprinkled by spoonfuls over the surface), then the bread crumbs combined with the baking powder.

Grease a 10-by-15-inch jelly-roll pan and line it with waxed paper. Pour in batter and bake 12 to 14 minutes. Remove from oven, invert on a clean kitchen towel, and roll the dough up with the towel jelly-roll fashion. Leave it rolled up and let it cool.

For the icing, beat to a light, fluffy consistency the unsalted butter with egg. Gradually add powdered sugar sifted together with cocoa. Add boiling water and blend. Spread this icing over the surface of the unrolled cake; roll it up and frost the outside. If you wish, add 1 or 2 tablespoons brandy or rum to the icing.

You may bake this same batter in two 8- or 9-inch round cake pans and make a two-layer chocolate nut torte. You may also omit the cocoa in the frosting, adding instead 6 tablespoons ground walnuts and 2 tablespoons rum, and decorate the slices with nut halves.

For a plain or nut torte, you may also use almonds, filberts (hazelnuts), pecans, or walnuts. The ratio remains the same.

When using this recipe to make a torte, use a springform pan, and always line it with waxed paper. After cooling, you may freeze layers for easier handling.

Note: You should never start to make a European recipe calling for ground nuts if you don't have the most important item — a European-style nut grinder that grinds the nuts into a fine nut flour without pressing the oil from them. A blender or food processor is not a satisfactory substitute. But it is not enough to grind the nutmeats properly. You also must fold them in by hand, with a plastic spatula. Don't "beat" the nuts into the mixture because the cake won't rise if you do.

GUGELHUPF
4 cups sifted flour
1 package active dry yeast
1/2 cup warm water
1/2 cup black currants and 1/2 cup white raisins, both soaked
for 10 minutes in boiling water, strained, then patted dry
on a towel and sprinkled with some flour
6 ounces butter, at room temperature
4 tablespoons powdered sugar
4 eggs, separated
1 pinch salt
1-1/2 to 2 cups milk
Zest of 1 lemon
Gugelhupf form

Activate the yeast by mixing it into the 1/2 cup warm water. Then bring 1/2 cup of the milk to a boil, let it cool to room temperature, add 2 to 3 tablespoons of the flour, and mix in the dissolved yeast. Let this sponge rise until it puffs and gets airy.

Place the butter in the bowl of an electric mixer and start beating at high speed. One by one, add the egg yolks and the salt. Beat until the mixture is fluffy and whipped.

Beat the egg whites, slowly adding the sugar, until they are stiff.

Stirring with a spatula, add the yeast mixture to the whipped butter mixture. Fold in the beaten egg whites, zest of the lemon, and remaining milk.

Sprinkle some of the flour over the top of the mixture and blend it in. Continue to sprinkle the flour on the top of the mixture and to blend it in until all of it is incorporated.

Sprinkle the black currants and raisins over the dough and gently fold them in. Brush a gugelhupf form with melted butter and dust it with flour. Pour the dough into the form and let it rise in a warm place until it is double in bulk.

Preheat the oven to 375 degrees. Bake the gugelhupf for approximately 45 to 60 minutes or until a testing needle, when inserted, comes out dry.

After baking, cool in the form. While still lukewarm, loosen the inner edges with a paring knife and invert to remove. Sprinkle the top generously with powdered sugar through a sieve. If possible, serve the next day.

This is one of several hundred gugelhupf recipes, each of which is claimed to be the one and only original Viennese recipe. This one is fairly easy to make, very tasty, and economical, and it can be kept in a cake container at room temperature for 3 to 4 days. The recipes Katharina Schratt used were considerably richer.

The gugelhupf may be glazed with chocolate, which makes it Gugelhupf à la Rothschild, or the greased form can be lined with slivered almonds, in which case it resembles the recipe Katharina Schratt's notebook called "Very good gugelhupf."

LINZER TORTE
1-1/4 cups flour
1-1/4 cups walnuts or almonds ground in a European-style nut grinder

1-3/4 cups butter
1 cup sugar
1 large egg
1/2 teaspoon baking powder
1/2 teaspoon cinnamon
1/2 teaspoon nutmeg
Pinch ground cloves
Grated zest of 1/2 lemon
2 8-inch cake pans
1 cup seedless black raspberry jam
1 cup red currant jelly
4 tablespoons powdered sugar
1 egg white
2 or 3 drops red food coloring
2 tablespoons chopped almonds
1 drop green food coloring
Grated rind of 1 lemon

Sift the flour into the middle of a pastry board or onto a clean, even-surfaced kitchen table so that the flour looks like a wide-based cone.

Make a well in the middle and add the sugar, ground nuts, baking powder, egg, spices, and grated lemon rind. If you wish, 2 or 3 tablespoons good brandy may be added to the dough.

Dust the surface of the butter with flour and start breaking the butter into small pieces, dipping your fingers into the flour before breaking each piece. Continue until all the pieces of butter are about the size of an almond or smaller.

Quickly mix the dough together with your fingertips, incorporating the flour from the outside into the middle.

Line the bottom of two 8-inch cake pans with waxed paper. Preheat the oven to 375 degrees. Divide the dough into three equal portions. Press one portion of dough into the bottom of each pan.

In a small saucepan over medium heat, melt the black raspberry jam and the red currant jelly together until the mixture comes to a boil. Stir and cook 5 to 6 minutes. Remove from heat and stir until it cools to lukewarm. Chill in the refrigerator, stirring occasionally. Once the mixture has chilled, divide it in half. Reserve half and spread the other half over the top of the dough in the two pans, dividing the mixture evenly.

Divide the third portion of dough in half. From each half, form strips 1/2 inch wide. Lay a diamond-shaped lace on the top of each pan with the strips of dough.

Bake the tortes 15 minutes. Reduce heat to 325 degrees and bake an additional 15 minutes. Cool. Cut around the edge of the tortes with a knife to loosen them from the pans, then remove.

Place the remaining jam mixture into a pastry bag fitted with a small star tube. Press some of the mixture into the diamond shapes, starting in the middle of both cakes and going in circles toward the edges, making sure you have enough jam mixture for each diamond.

Note that the baking powder in this recipe is only an insurance policy for the beginner. When you have mastered the technique of working rapidly with the dough so as to keep the butter from melting, you may omit it.

If you would like to have a very colorful, ornate-looking torte, you may decorate it as follows. In a small bowl, stir the powdered sugar and egg white with a few drops of red food coloring until it turns into a smooth pink substance. Pipe this substance around the rims of the Linzer Tortes. Return them to a 200-degree oven for 15 minutes to dry. Next, with your fingertips, mix the chopped almonds with green food coloring so that all the pieces of almonds become somewhat greenish. Sprinkle the almonds over the top of each torte. Or you may sprinkle chopped pistachio nuts over the tortes. Store the tortes at least 2 days before serving.

Work very fast with this dough to avoid "burning" it with your fingertips. Professional pastry chefs roll the dough for the lattice into ropelike pieces by hand, but this is difficult. It will be easier to roll out the dough on a pastry board dusted with a little flour, then cut the strips with a knife or with a round-bladed pastry or crinkle cutter.

STRUDEL

Nowadays excellent commercial strudel dough is available frozen throughout the United States. In most larger cities, especially those with a Greek population, filo leaves are also available fresh, refrigerated, and frozen.

If you are an absolute purist and must make your own strudel dough, here is the recipe. But I have to warn you: Don't try to make strudel the first time in your life for guests on the day of the party. Strudel dough is really one of the simplest doughs to make *if* you master the technique and have had a chance to try the best available flours. The flour must be very dry, smooth, all-purpose flour, if possible from a Canadian durum type of grain, such as the Four Roses flour which is available in many parts of the United States.

For the Dough

3 cups flour
Pinch of salt
1-1/2 tablespoons lard
1 medium egg
1 teaspoon plain white vinegar
1 to 1-1/4 cups lukewarm water
1 tablespoon farina

Sift the flour onto a pastry board in a cone shape. Make a well in the middle, and place in the well the salt, lard, egg, vinegar, and a little bit of the lukewarm water. With your fingertips, start to work all the soft ingredients into the flour, adding small amounts of water until all the flour can be gathered into one mass. First it will be sticky, but as you work the dough will turn very elastic with air bubbles in it.

Form the dough into a ball, sprinkle a corner of the pastry board with a very little flour, place the ball on it, pat it down somewhat, and, with your fingertips, brush the top with a very small amount of lard. Then cover the ball with a saucepan that has been warmed over medium heat.

Let it stand for 20 to 25 minutes or even longer. Have all your fillings ready at hand before you start to work with the dough.

Cover a large table with a tablecloth, dust the tablecloth with 3 to 4 tablespoons flour mixed with 1 tablespoon farina.

Now, with your fingers, brush the dough with a little bit of lard and start to pull it first to the left and then to the right. After a little pulling, go under the dough with your fist and try to pull it over your fist from the middle toward the two edges at once. If the dough is good, it will start to get thin. Then, holding it very gently with your fingers and being very careful not to make a hole in it with your fingernails, start to lift and pull the dough all over the table, walking around the table in the same direction. You have to use the kind of waving movement that you would use to straighten out a blanket over a bed. Pull the dough until it is so large that it hangs off the table all around. Cut off the excess hanging dough and let the thin strudel dough dry for 10 minutes or so.

Now start to fill the strudel: Melt 1/2 cup unsalted butter and sprinkle the surface of the dough with butter. Then sprinkle the whole surface with about 1/2 cup of fine, dry bread crumbs mixed with 1/2 cup ground almonds or ground walnuts. Spread the filling the long way on about one-third of the strudel dough. Holding the tablecloth, start to roll up the strudel dough, jelly-roll fashion. Keep sprinkling with melted butter as it turns and keep rolling until all the dough is rolled up. Now cut the strudel into the length of your cookie sheet, brush the cookie sheet and the top of the strudel with melted butter, and transfer the strudel to the cookie sheet with a long metal spatula or a long knife.

Bake in a very hot oven (400–425 degrees) 25 to 45 minutes, depending on the amount and kind of strudel.

Warning: I repeat, this is not an easy technique, but it is possible to learn. In Hungary, Austria, the former Yugoslavia, and many other countries, hundreds of thousands of cooks do it, but first you must learn before you can excel.

POPPY SEED STRUDEL FILLING

2 cups fresh poppy seeds, passed through a special poppy seed grinder
(see the List of Vendors)
1 cup raisins, soaked and patted dry

1 cup sugar
1/2 cup honey
Milk
Zest of 1/2 lemon and 1/2 orange, grated

Soak 1 cup raisins in 4 cups boiling water, not over the fire, for 30 minutes. Pat the raisins dry and add them to the ground poppy seeds. Add 1 cup sugar, 1/2 cup honey; cook with enough regular milk to cover, over slow heat, until the mixture begins to thicken. As the mixture cools, add the grated rind of 1/2 lemon and 1/2 orange. When the mixture is completely cool, it can be used to fill a strudel.

CABBAGE STRUDEL FILLING

Melted lard or other shortening for brushing
4-pound head of cabbage, cored and finely chopped
1/2 cup shortening
1 tablespoon grated onion
2 teaspoons salt
1 teaspoon freshly ground black pepper
4 tablespoons sugar

Preheat oven to 325 degrees.

Chop the cabbage so that the pieces are no bigger than oatmeal flakes. In a large skillet, melt 1/2 cup shortening, such as bacon drippings, lard, or oil. Add grated or finely minced onion. Add the cabbage and sprinkle on the salt, freshly ground black pepper, and sugar.

Sauté gently over medium heat, stirring occasionally, until the mixture turns light gold and limp and loses about half of its volume. Keep stirring to avoid scorching. Add more fat if you think the mixture is drying out.

Remove from heat and let cool until lukewarm. Place cooled filling onto strudel dough and roll up. Bake in a hot oven for 20 to 25 minutes.

NAPOLEON SLICES

1 package frozen filo leaves or strudel leaves
1 cup melted butter

1/2 cup very fine white bread crumbs
1/2 cup granulated sugar
1 recipe Basic Vanilla Cream
3 eggs
1 pint heavy cream
3 tablespoons sugar
1 pinch salt
1 envelope unflavored gelatin
3 tablespoons cold water
1/2 cup water
Powdered sugar

Defrost and handle the filo or strudel leaves according to the package directions. In the meantime, make the Basic Vanilla Cream and allow it to cool. Lightly brush 2 cookie sheets (each large enough to hold a piece of dough approximately 12 by 16 inches) with some of the melted butter.

Mix the bread crumbs with the 1/2 cup sugar. Lay two filo or strudel leaves on each cookie sheet. With a pastry brush, generously sprinkle the leaves with some of the melted butter, then evenly sprinkle each with some of the bread crumb–sugar mixture. Repeat this process four times on each sheet, so that you have eight leaves on each.

With the tip of a small paring knife, gently cut fine incisions in the pastry and bake it in a preheated 375- to 400-degree oven for 4 to 5 minutes. Remove and let the pastry cool.

Separate the eggs. In a large bowl, combine the Basic Vanilla Cream with the 3 egg yolks, which have been slightly beaten with a fork. Beat the egg whites until they are stiff but not dry.

Soften the gelatin in the 3 tablespoons water. Bring the 1/2 cup water to a boil and dissolve the softened gelatin in the boiling water. Cool by setting the pan in an ice-water bath until the gelatin is syrupy.

Whip the heavy cream, adding the pinch of salt and the sugar. Fold the beaten egg whites into the stiffly beaten cream. Add the cooled, syrupy gelatin and fold in with a spatula, distributing the gelatin throughout the mixture. Fold into the Vanilla Cream mixture.

Evenly pile this mixture on one of the pastry sheets. Place in the freezer to chill until firm.

With a wet, sharp knife, cut the filling and bottom pastry into serving-size pieces. Cut the other baked pastry sheet into pieces of the same size and place these pieces on top of the precut filling and bottom layer. Chill in the refrigerator.

Just before serving, dust the top of the Napoleon slices with powdered sugar.

Note: To make it easier to distribute the filling neatly, make a frame to hold it in place: Cut four pieces of cardboard, making two of them 12-1/4 inches long and two 16-1/4 inches long. Tape the four pieces together, then cover them with aluminum foil and tape the foil on the outside. Place this foil frame around the bottom strudel pastry sheet after baking it, before you pour the filling over it. The filling will not run and will be evenly distributed over the surface. To remove the frame, simply heat a dull knife in hot water, run the knife around the inner edge of the frame, and lift it off.

BASIC VANILLA CREAM

1 quart milk

1/2 cup sugar

1/2 teaspoon salt

1 teaspoon vanilla extract

3 egg yolks

8 teaspoons cornstarch

3 ounces butter

Dissolve the cornstarch in 1 cup of the milk. Beat the egg yolks slightly with a fork and add them to the milk-cornstarch mixture.

Place the remaining 3 cups of milk in a medium-sized saucepan. Add the sugar, salt, vanilla, and butter. Start to heat this mixture, stirring to dissolve the sugar.

Once the mixture begins to boil, start to stir with a wire whip and pour in the milk–cornstarch–egg yolk mixture. You will have to beat this mixture very vigorously with the wire whip as it will become very stiff. It will not be necessary to cook more than 5 minutes; the mixture will thicken almost immediately.

Remove from the heat as soon as the cream is smooth and thick. Let cool.

HAZELNUT BREAD

4 ounces sugar

8 yolks

4 ounces ground hazelnuts

3 ounces grated chocolate

4 beaten egg whites

1-1/2 ounces bread crumbs

In an electric mixer, beat 4 ounces sugar and 8 egg yolks until lemon-colored and fluffy. Add 4 ounces ground hazelnuts spoonful by spoonful, gently folding with a rubber spatula after each addition, then fold in the 3 ounces grated chocolate in the same way. Fold in beaten egg whites, 1-1/2 ounces bread crumbs. Bake in a buttered and floured loaf pan at 325 degrees for about 25 minutes or until a cake tester comes out clean.

SICILIAN CAKE

1 recipe Linzer Torte dough (see p. 187)

1 pint milk

3 ounces sugar

4 yolks

1 egg

Vanilla

Cinnamon

3 tablespoons rum

2 ounces flour

First prepare Linzer Torte Dough according to the recipe on page 187. Divide in half. Use half for Sicilian Cake and second half for a linzer torte.

Use two-thirds of the half portion of linzer dough to line a 9-inch springform pan, as you would do for a linzer torte. Separate 4 eggs, setting aside the whites for other purposes. In a small bowl combine with a wire whisk the milk, sugar, yolks, and whole egg. When this mixture is well combined, transfer it to a small saucepan and keep beating over medium heat. Add 1 teaspoon vanilla extract or the inside pulp and seeds from 1-1/2 inches vanilla bean, a pinch of cinnamon, and the rum. While continuing to beat the mixture, slowly sift the 2 ounces of flour onto it. Continue beating until the mixture comes to a boil. Then remove it from the heat and continue beating until it cools. When the mixture has cooled, pour it onto the linzer dough in the springform pan and let it set. Use the remaining linzer dough to make a lattice for the top of the Sicilian Cake. Bake at 300 degrees for about 30 minutes. Serve warm.

PIQUANT FRUIT (FRENCH)

8−10 pineapple slices
2 large or 3 medium oranges, peeled, finely sliced
1 pint heavy cream
2 tablespoons vanilla sugar
6−8 teaspoons kirsch liqueur
6−8 teaspoons maraschino liqueur .
1 pint strawberries, cleaned, hulled, cross sliced
8−10 large grapes, sliced in half

For 8−10 persons, take 8−10 pineapple slices. Cut the slices very fine and place them in a shallow bowl. Then add a layer of finely sliced oranges. Whip a pint of heavy cream, add vanilla sugar, 6−8 teaspoons kirsch, 6−8 teaspoons maraschino liqueur. Pour this mixture over the fruit, decorate with strawberries and grapes. Put the dish on ice and serve it cold.

NOODLES À LA ÖDENBURG

1 recipe Noodle Pudding (see p. 197)
1 cup poppy seeds, ground through a poppy seed mill
2 tablespoons butter
3 tablespoons sugar
1 pinch cinnamon
2 teaspoons lemon zest
1 cup milk

Prepare a good noodle pudding. Place half of it in an ovenproof dish and bake lightly. Over this spread the poppy seed filling sautéed in butter with the sugar, cinnamon, and lemon zest blended with a cup of milk. Top with the other half of the noodle pudding, dot with some additional butter, and bake in a slow oven.

NOODLE PUDDING

4 tablespoons melted butter
1 pound broad noodles, boiled and drained
4 eggs, separated
1 teaspoon ground cinnamon
1/4 teaspoon ground nutmeg
1-1/4 cups sugar
1/4 teaspoon salt
1 cup raisins
Jelly or jam (optional)

Preheat the oven to 350 degrees.

Add the melted butter to the noodles. Beat the egg yolks with the sugar; blend in the spices and the salt. Add to the noodles.

Beat the egg whites until stiff but not dry. Fold the egg whites into the noodles. Pour one-third of the mixture into a 2-quart baking dish. Sprinkle one-half of the raisins and nuts in. Add another third of the noodle mixture, the remaining nuts and raisins, and then the rest of the noodle mixture.

Bake in the preheated oven for 45 minutes or until set. Serve hot. If you like, offer warmed and diluted jelly or jam. The success of the Noodle Pudding depends greatly on a very light hand and on the speed with which you can complete the steps. The best way to mix the egg yolk–sugar mixture into the noodles is to pour the mixture directly from the mixing bowl over the noodles, which must be dripped perfectly dry, and then to fold them together gently with a rubber spatula. The same method should be used for the addition of the egg whites.

If you want to unmold the Noodle Pudding before serving, brush the inside of the baking dish with butter or oil and sprinkle it generously with bread crumbs mixed with a little bit of sugar before pouring the pudding in.

If the raisins are not especially fresh, soak them a short time in lukewarm water, but do not plump them; plumping will make them lose their taste and texture.

SACHER TORTE

3/4 cup butter
6 fresh large eggs which have been separated and kept at
room temperature
2 cups sifted cake flour
3/4 cup sugar
1 teaspoon vanilla extract
6 squares (6 ounces) unsweetened chocolate, melted and cooled

In an electric mixer, cream the butter until it starts to fluff. Add the sugar slowly, keep mixing until well blended. Add the egg yolks, one at a time, being careful not to include any of the white. Beat after each addition until the egg yolk is incorporated. Add the vanilla. Add about one-third of the flour, folding it in gently with a rubber spatula.

In another bowl whip the egg whites until stiff. Fold a small part of the egg whites into the cooled melted chocolate. Then combine this chocolate–egg white mixture with the rest of the egg whites. Now combine the egg white mixture and the egg yolk mixture and slowly fold in the remaining flour. Divide the batter between two buttered and floured 9-inch springform pans and bake at 350 degrees for approximately 25 to 30 minutes. Cool. Warm 4 tablespoons apricot jam with 3 tablespoons liquid of your choice, such as orange juice, rum, sherry, lemon juice if you like it tart, etc. Brush both layers with this glaze. Coat with a simple chocolate glaze as follows:

Melt 6 to 8 ounces semi-sweet chocolate pieces in the top of a double boiler. Add 1 tablespoon sweet butter. Stir and quickly pour it over the layers, smoothing it with a warm knife.

EMPEROR'S TRIFLE

1/2 cup raisins
1-3/4 cups sifted flour
3 cups milk

4 eggs, separated
3 or 4 tablespoons confectioners' sugar
Grated zest (yellow rind only) of 1 lemon
1/4 cup melted butter
Pinch of salt
1/2 cup butter mixed with 1/2 cup shortening for frying
Confectioners' sugar

Soak raisins in hot water for 30 minutes, then pat dry.

In a bowl, stir flour and milk together with a wire whisk. Add egg yolks, 2 tablespoons confectioners' sugar, grated lemon zest, and 1/4 cup melted butter. Mix until smooth.

Beat egg whites with a pinch of salt until very stiff and shiny. Don't overbeat. Fold into batter.

Heat half of butter and shortening mixture in a frying pan. When very hot, pour in half the batter and start to cook it as you would a large pancake. Keep lifting edges with two forks, letting runny batter seep under edges. When completely set, tear pancake into four quarters with two forks, turn each quarter, and cook on other side. Remove from pan. Add remaining butter and shortening to pan, heat it, and repeat procedure with remaining batter.

Tear all pancake quarters into pieces the size of a quarter or smaller. Mix with raisins and heat quickly in pan, turning constantly. Pile onto a serving platter and dust with remaining confectioners' sugar. Serve with a fresh fruit sauce, such as Fresh Plum Sauce.

FRESH PLUM SAUCE

Pit 1 pound Italian plums. Cut each pitted plum into 4 or more pieces. In a saucepan, bring 4 cups of water to a boil with 2 tablespoons sugar, the juice of 1/2 lemon, and a 1-by-2-inch piece of lemon rind, 2 or 3 whole cloves, and a 2-inch piece of cinnamon bark. As soon as mixture boils, add cut-up plums. Stir and bring to a boil again. Remove from heat, cover, and let stand at least 10 minutes. Remove lemon rind, cloves, and cinnamon bark. Serve warm sauce in a sauceboat and let guests serve themselves by spooning sauce over pastry.

APPENDIX

VIENNESE CUISINE AND HEALTH

In the introduction to this section, I mentioned the fact that our tastes have changed since the time of Katharina Schratt. As a result of our broadened understanding of nutrition, our daily diet is dominated by fresh fruit and vegetables and other complex carbohydrates. Many of us avoid meat, at least to some degree, and very many of us shy away from fats and oils to a dramatic extent. All of these things make sense, but they do not exclude the possibility of an occasional adventure that explores another culture and its way of eating. (I do not say life-style, because you probably wouldn't want to walk up and down as many stairs or carry as many scuttles full of coal or wake up to the chilly winter bedrooms inhabited by the people who cooked and ate this food.)

The biggest danger of foods such as fats, for instance, or refined sugars is habitual consumption, not the very occasional treat. Therefore, I would like to make this suggestion to the American cook who comes along with me to try these recipes. Please do not try to make substitutions that seem to you to make these recipes "healthier." If you are clever in the kitchen, your substitution may work, to the extent that the finished product looks right. But nine times out of ten it won't taste like the real thing; it will taste "lite." Make it a special occasion! Cook well, dine with gusto with your friends and family, then go for a brisk walk and eat lots of celery tomorrow!

CHEF'S SALT

It is a fact that in our society much more salt is consumed than necessary. But certainly healthy people who have no dietary restrictions should have a little salt, and it is important to know how to make a little salt go a long way. First of all, salt should be added early in the cooking process. I am a violent opponent of salt-free food because I don't ever want anyone to oversalt good food. If you cook a dish for four to six people, the salt added in the beginning will be less than what each eater will add to unsalted food at the dining table. What's more, you can cut down on salt by mixing a Chef's Salt, a combination of flavors that you can make your own. One simple recipe is:

1 cup salt
1 tablespoon Hungarian paprika
1 teaspoon freshly ground black pepper
1/4 teaspoon ground white pepper
1/4 teaspoon garlic salt

Be careful to use garlic salt, not garlic powder. If you use garlic powder, a small pinch is enough. Mix well and store in a covered jar.

If you add this mixture instead of plain salt, you will be pleasantly surprised. Each food, chicken or beef or cauliflower, will taste more like itself. A good Chef's Salt is like a basic scale in music; if Mozart and Beethoven and rap singers can all compose their masterpieces on the same scale from C to C, there should be no reason why the most various effects of flavor cannot be composed within the same "spice-scale" system. A few bay leaves, some rosemary, a pinch of mustard, a dollop of anchovy paste, and the taste is your own.

MAYONNAISE

2 large or 3 medium egg yolks
2/3 teaspoon salt
Small pinch white pepper
Few grains cayenne pepper
4 teaspoons sugar

2 *tablespoons plus 2 teaspoons white vinegar*

1-1/2 *cups corn oil (or olive oil, if you wish)*

4 *teaspoons lemon juice*

1 *to 2 tablespoons boiling water*

Place the egg yolks in a mixing bowl and add the salt, white pepper, cayenne pepper, sugar, and vinegar. Using an electric mixer (a must for this recipe), beat the yolks and seasonings at the highest speed for 2 to 3 minutes or until the mixture turns pale yellow and liquid. Adjust the speed to medium and add the oil, first drop by drop, then in a thin stream. When the oil is thoroughly combined, set the mixer on low speed and add the lemon juice and boiling water. Store the mayonnaise in the refrigerator in a plastic or glass container.

Mayonnaise is a formula more than a hundred years old, and there is very little variation in its preparation, but certain points must be stressed.

All utensils, especially the mixing bowl and beaters, must be absolutely clean and free of grease and moisture. Therefore, rinse them with a boiling mixture of 3 cups water and 1 cup vinegar. Then rinse under a large amount of cold running water and dry with a fresh, clean kitchen towel. If the bowl and beaters are not completely dry, the mayonnaise will not be perfect.

Sometimes the mayonnaise breaks down despite the best care in preparation. To reconstitute, just use the absolutely clean and dry mixer and start to beat the mayonnaise on the lowest speed. Slowly increase the speed to medium and add 1/3 to 1/2 cup extra oil, pouring in a very thin stream. The best way to assure a thin stream is to pour the oil from a spouted container, held 15 to 18 inches from the top of the mixing bowl.

Champagne Mayonnaise: Add 3 tablespoons champagne for each cup of mayonnaise and omit the boiling water.

Green Mayonnaise: Chop very fine 1 cup of green parsley and place it in a wet kitchen towel. Gather towel so that the parsley resembles a ball. Squeeze the parsley juice into a small dish. Add 2 to 3 tablespoons to 1 cup mayonnaise.

BREAD CRUMBS

Commercially available bread crumbs are sometimes stale or rancid, which is nobody's fault. It is best to make your own bread crumbs.

Be sure to purchase a French or Italian type of bread and carefully read the list of ingredients. It should not contain any type of shortening. Flour, water, salt, and yeast are the ingredients of real Italian, French, or Vienna bread.

Air dry the loaf 2 to 3 days, perhaps in a cheesecloth bag, then slice it thick. Roll to crumbs with a rolling pin and sift. Or, if you wish, grate the slices on a four-sided kitchen grater.

Keep the crumbs in a container, but not airtight. And don't keep them too long. It is much less expensive to throw out a quarter's worth of bread crumbs than a dollar's worth of Wiener schnitzel.

PARISIAN SPICE (Pâté Spice)

1 tablespoon crushed bay leaf
1 tablespoon dried thyme
1 tablespoon powdered mace
1 tablespoon dried rosemary
1 tablespoon dried basil
2 tablespoons cinnamon
1-1/2 teaspoons ground cloves
1/2 teaspoon ground nutmeg
1/2 teaspoon ground allspice
1 teaspoon ground white pepper
2 teaspoons Spanish paprika
1 cup salt

Mix all ingredients well in a spice mortar or crush them together in a deep bowl with the bottom of a cup. Sift through a fine sieve 2 or 3 times, crush again, and sift until everything goes through. Keep in a tightly covered jar.

BROWN STOCK

1 pound chicken necks or backs
2 to 3 pounds beef shank with bone in, cut into 1-inch slices

2 cups chopped carrots
1 cup chopped white or yellow turnip
1 large leek washed and split in half lengthwise, washed again,
then sliced into 1/2-inch strips and washed again
1/2 cup chopped parsley root or parsnip
2 medium onions, skin on, cut crosswise at the root,
and stuck with a clove
2 pounds lean ground beef
5 quarts water
3 to 4 tablespoons salt
1 teaspoon black peppercorns crushed or bruised
4 ribs celery tied with 1 bay leaf and 4 to 5 sprigs parsley
1 clove garlic with skin on, halved

Preheat oven to 375 degrees.

Place the chicken backs and necks and the beef shank in a not-too-deep roasting pan and, depending on the size of the pan, place it over one or two burners of the stove top. Add half of each of the carrots, turnip, leek, and parsley root, and one onion. Keep turning the bones and the sliced shank so that they brown. Move the vegetables around, preferably with a wooden spoon, until they start to brown, then remove from heat. Distribute the ground beef over the pan and pour 5 quarts of cold water over the mixture.

Add salt, black peppercorns, celery ribs with bay leaf and parsley, garlic, and the second onion, and bake uncovered about 3 hours. Remove and strain the liquid.

Put all bones, meat, vegetables, and remaining raw vegetables into a large (at least 3-gallon) soup pot. Add enough cold water to the cooking liquid to have exactly 5 quarts again. Pour the 5 quarts of liquid over the other ingredients, bring to a gentle boil, and then adjust heat to low and simmer for at least 4 hours, preferably longer.

Just before removing from heat, add 2 cups of cold water with 1 cup of ice cubes in it. This will help bring all the fat to the top of the liquid. Skim as much fat as possible and let the stock stand without stirring for about an hour. Then dip a kitchen towel in lukewarm water, soak it for a minute or two, squeeze it (not too dry), place it over a sieve or colander, and without disturbing the solids in the pot gently pour the liquid through the kitchen towel and colander into another container. Cool quickly and store. If you end up with less than 4 quarts, add enough water to make 4 quarts.

For twice the amount of stock, add just one half more of all ingredients, that is, 1-1/2 pounds chicken backs and necks, 3 to 4 pounds beef shank, 3 cups carrots, etc., and proceed as for the basic recipe.

WHITE STOCK

2 to 3 pounds beef shank, bone in, cut into 1-inch slices
3 to 4 pounds veal front, neck or breast, cut into small pieces
2 to 3 pounds chicken necks, wing tips, or backs
1 cup chopped carrots
1 cup chopped turnip
1 leek washed, split lengthwise, washed again, cut crosswise
into 1/2-inch pieces, and washed again
1/2 cup chopped parsley root or parsnip
1 medium onion, peeled and chopped
1 clove
2 or 3 celery ribs tied with 2 or 3 sprigs of parsley
and 1 bay leaf
4 tablespoons salt
12 peppercorns, bruised or crushed
6 quarts cold water

Place all ingredients, including water, in a large stock pot. Bring to a boil; skim off the white scum from the top. Set heat very low and simmer for at least 4, preferably 6, hours.

Remove from heat and add 2 cups of cold water with a cup of ice cubes to bring the grease to the top. Skim off the grease and let the stock pot stand for about an hour on a wire rack.

Skim off remaining fat. Place a colander in a clean, cold, metal container. Line the colander with a moist but not wet kitchen towel and ladle the stock through it into the container. If it is less than 4 quarts, add enough water to make 4 quarts. Cool and use immediately or store for later use.

These two recipes for stocks are basic and, of course, can be improved if you add herbs or spices of your choice. If you want the brown stock to be darker, simply add a tablespoon or so of Kitchen Bouquet or Gravy Master. Or grate a 2-inch length of carrot into a small pan, add 1 tablespoon shortening and 1 tablespoon sugar, and cook over high heat until carrots and sugar start to brown. Remove, add 2 or 3 tablespoons hot water or hot stock, and strain the carrot caramel juice into the stock.

If you want the white stock to be golden yellow like chicken stock, follow the same procedure, omitting the sugar and heating only the carrots in the shortening.

Both stocks can be frozen in an ice cube tray. Pack each cube individually in aluminum foil or plastic and then put them in a plastic bag or container. Do not keep frozen longer than a month.

BEEF STOCK

8 ounces slab bacon
4 pounds beef bones
2 or 3 onions, depending on size, skin on
2 cloves garlic, unpeeled
2 to 3 carrots, coarsely chopped
2 cups coarsely chopped celery tops
1 leek or 2 or 3 scallions
1 bunch (12 to 15 sprigs) green parsley
1 parsley root or parsnip
About 8 ounces turnip or rutabaga
2 to 3 tablespoons salt
1 teaspoon black peppercorns
1 bay leaf
3 to 4 whole cloves
1 pound beef shank
2 pounds veal front or veal bones
1 tablespoon tomato paste

Cut into the top surface of the slab bacon crosswise, cutting about two-thirds of the way to the rind. Put the bacon and beef bones in a large skillet. Over medium to high heat, render the fat from the bacon. When there is a layer of hot fat in the bottom of the pan, cut each onion in half, crosswise, and place cut-surface down in the fat. Fry until deep dark brown.

Remove and discard bacon and place the garlic, carrots, celery tops, leek, parsley, parsley root, and turnip in the pan on top of the bones, which should be somewhat brown on the surface. Add salt, peppercorns, bay leaf, and cloves. Stir for a couple of minutes, then let the vegetables brown slightly.

Place the beef shank and veal front, cut into two or three pieces, in a large soup pot. Transfer all the contents of the skillet to the pot. Add water to a level of 2 inches above the solid ingredients. Add the tomato paste. Cover and bring to a boil. Reduce heat to low and simmer, covered, for at least 6 hours. Remove from heat and let stand 1 hour.

Skim and discard all fat from the pot. Pour liquid through a colander to another pot, pressing vegetable gently to remove liquid. Discard all bones and vegetables.

Chop the meat from the bones, beef shank, and veal front, then grind it through a meat grinder and return it to the stock pot. Again bring the stock to a boil, reduce heat, cover, and simmer about 2 hours. Let stand 1 hour, skim surface to remove fat, then strain through a wet kitchen towel. Correct seasoning by adding more salt if necessary. Makes 4 quarts.

This is a basic stock recipe suitable for a homemaker. It may, of course, be varied by omitting certain spices or vegetables or by adding others. If you don't wish to use bacon, replace with a piece of suet.

The veal front contains a very large amount of natural gelatin which boils out, dissolves in the stock, and adds to its viscosity or makes it syrupy. The bacon with the rind left on also helps in this regard, since a large amount of natural gelatin cooks out from the bacon rind.

If you want to store this stock for later use, the best and easiest way is as follows: Measure the amount of stock you have. If, for instance, it is 3 quarts, pour 1-1/2 quarts water into an empty pot. Use a wooden spoon to measure the depth of the water in the pan, making a mark on the spoon. Discard water and pour the stock into the same pan. Simmer slowly, uncovered, until half of it evaporates or until the liquid level in the pan is the same as it was with the 1-1/2 quarts of water. Cool the reduced liquid, then pour into ice cube trays and freeze. Wrap each stock cube individually in plastic wrap and store in the freezer. When you need a little stock, take out one cube and dilute with an equal amount of water. You can do the same thing with any other stock or cooking liquid such as fish, chicken, veal, or ham stock.

SAUCE ESPAGNOLE

(BASIC BROWN SAUCE)

4 tablespoons melted butter

2 tablespoons lard, bacon drippings, or rendered suet

4 tablespoons flour

1 tablespoon cornstarch

2 tablespoons tomato puree

1 teaspoon Worcestershire sauce

Grinding of fresh black pepper

4 cups beef stock

Melt the butter and other shortening in a saucepan. Stir the flour, cornstarch, tomato puree, Worcestershire sauce, and pepper into 1 cup of the stock. Using a wire whip and stirring vigorously, blend this mixture into the melted shortening, cooking over medium heat. As soon as the mixture starts to thicken, immediately begin to add the remaining 3 cups stock, pouring in a thin stream and stirring until completely incorporated.

Cook over medium heat 3 to 4 minutes, stirring occasionally. Reduce the heat to low and scrape the bottom and sides of the pan with a plastic or rubber spatula so that no thick parts adhere to the pan and the whole mixture is of an even consistency.

Simmer at least 1 hour over very low heat. Correct seasoning by adding a very little sugar if too acidic or salt if too mild. Makes 4 cups.

In all older cookbooks and even in some of today's European cookbooks, you will find entirely different recipes for Sauce Espagnole (Basic Brown Sauce). They will all start by making a roux, stirring the flour into the shortening, and cooking until it turns brown, stirring continuously. This method was essential in the eighteenth and nineteenth centuries because of the lack of refrigeration and dry storage. If the two basic ingredients were not cooked together, the shortening would go rancid and the flour would mildew. So the ingredients were cooked to keep them usable for several days or even a week.

Of course, for a twentieth-century chef or homemaker with a refrigerator, freezer, and good storage, it is silly to spend hours to make a concoction designed to prevent spoilage. Thus making Sauce Espagnole is no longer the chore it used to be.

Sauce Espagnole must be simmered for a long time over low heat so that its flavor will blend. This is essential whether the sauce is to be used alone or as a base for other sauces.

MADEIRA SAUCE

To make madeira sauce, add 1/2 cup to 1 cup madeira, depending on the quality of the wine, to Sauce Espagnole. For egg dishes with goose liver which need a pronounced taste, I would use 3 tablespoons madeira sauce per egg with an extra teaspoon of wine in the sauce.

BÉCHAMEL SAUCE

1/4 cup butter
2 tablespoons flour
1 tablespoon cornstarch
1 cup light cream
1 can (10-1/2 ounces) chicken stock
Salt
White pepper

In a medium-sized, heavy-bottomed saucepan, heat the butter over medium heat until it starts to foam. Dissolve the flour and cornstarch in the light cream, mixing until well blended. Pour this into the foaming butter, stirring constantly, until the sauce has thickened. Adjust heat so that the sauce does not scorch. Stir in the chicken stock and continue to cook over low heat for at least 5 minutes. Season well with salt and pepper. Strain.

If the chicken stock is not strong enough, add half a chicken bouillon cube and a very small amount of celery seed. If you want an exceptional béchamel, finish it just before serving as follows: Stiffly whip 1/2 to 1 cup whipping cream with a pinch of salt. Tablespoonful by tablespoonful, fold some of the hot béchamel into the whipped cream to warm it gradually, then fold the whipped cream mixture into the sauce. Serve immediately. Don't use a wire whip for this folding; a rubber or plastic spatula works best.

This sauce is very versatile and can be easily varied with the addition of small amounts of concentrated flavoring. For instance, it makes an exceptional sauce for fish, fowl, or veal with the addition of 1 tablespoon anchovy paste and 1 tablespoon rinsed capers. (Always rinse capers under running cold water before using, to get rid of the chemical taste of the liquid from the jar.) Or you can add 1 to 2 tablespoons French mustard with 1 heaping teaspoon curry powder, or 1 ripe banana mashed with a fork together with 1 teaspoon curry powder, or 2 tablespoons grated Parmesan and 2 tablespoons grated Swiss cheese, or 3 to 4 tablespoons processed cheese grated with 1 or 2 tablespoons Parmesan.

❧ LIST OF VENDORS ❧

I have assembled this last section for readers who want to learn more about the history, culture, sociology, and economy of Vienna at the turn of the century by working with its cuisine. Some of you yearn to recapture the delectable smells you remember from the family kitchen; others, with a different heritage, may just be very curious about some of the names and all of the praise that surrounds this culinary tradition. For most of you, various impediments might seem to stand in your way as you consider trying the recipes in this section or other recipes straight from the original. Most of you find that time is your most precious commodity and can't spare too much of it in the kitchen. Some of you may live far away from a large city with a strong, old central European tradition that demands shops with the right ingredients and equipment. Or perhaps you hesitate to try cooking something that seems complicated or very unfamiliar.

These are some of the reasons why I am providing a list of vendors from whom both food and equipment can be obtained. These companies do not just supply merchandise. They are links in the chain of information and tradition stretching from the past to the future. Working with them, you will be able to make use of scratch ingredients or modern tricks (no one has to know!) to make a marvelous chicken soup, a great Tafelspitz, a wonderful pudding, or a fine appetizer that brings back memories of childhood or your honeymoon or other once-in-a-lifetime trips to Central Europe. No one who is enjoying the delectable food you have made will quiz you about how you managed this little masterpiece.

When you are working against the clock, I hope that instead of thinking you have no hope of making a great brown stock or a wonderful complex sauce which tastes authentic through simmering and reusing and simmering and reusing for hours and hours, you will try reaching for a teaspoonful of a soup base created to save time and effort. In the same way, I hope you remember that if you want the inimitable mouth feel, fragrance, and taste of a poppy seed strudel, you'll take account of the fact that you can do it both ways. You can either buy a poppy seed grinder, fresh poppy seeds, soak the raisins, simmer the cream, grate the lemon rind, and cut the apples fine or you can open a can of prepared, ready-to-use poppy seed filling.

I don't want to suggest that the reader who turns into a doer or the food enthusiast who turns into a cook should find substitutes for ingredients and methods, but I want to give those whose time is precious the opportunity to be able to re-create, through the wonders of modern ingredients, equipment, and methods, the old sensations of the taste buds and olfactory organs.

And why *should* you spend your time calling around and going around looking for the unique ingredient, the out-of-the-ordinary smoked meat, the special canned good, or whatever you need, when I can help you obtain it quickly and in the small quantities that a home kitchen needs? Many of the sources listed here helped me to be in the restaurant business for more than a quarter of a century. As a result, I came to understand and believe firmly what Auguste Escoffier, the chef of kings and king of chefs, repeated throughout his career: "The chef should not get more than 60 percent of the praise and compliments for the finest meal. At least another 40 percent is due to the suppliers."

Aside from all the important fresh foods we were so careful to obtain for our restaurant, we made our soup excellent and extraordinary by using the most reputable and best soup bases to boost their richness, fragrance, and aroma, and our spices were splendid because we purchased them from a small local supplier who had his Muntock peppers shipped from Madagascar, his black pepper from the most reputable wholesaler in India, and his paprika transported by air from Hungary to Chicago to preserve its vivid color and incomparable aroma.

I give you here fewer than two dozen suppliers from the several thousand available, from the several hundred I contacted and checked out from coast to coast. I hope that this legwork will help you to enjoy interesting, rewarding, and successful meals and will open a world of food information which will help you to get closer, both as a reader and as a doer, to the food ways, culture, and civilization of the Central Europe of the turn of the century and of today.

Allserv
Post Office Box 43209
Cleveland, OH 44143-0209
800/827-8328   Fax: 216/486-9868

Contact: Mr. and Mrs. David Seivers

The sole distributor, to consumers, of Minor bases, the largest variety of the highest quality soup and sauce bases. These bases are used by leading restaurants to intensify and enhance soups and sauces. They are now available in 8-ounce containers. Call for more information.

Bende & Son Salami Co., Inc.

875 Corporate Woods Parkway

Vernon Hills, IL 60061

708/913-0304

Bende manufactures a wide variety of Hungarian-style smoked meats. In addition, the company offers an impressive array of Hungarian pastas, jams, preserves, pickled peppers, sweet and hot paprika, to name a few of their treasures. To place an order, write or call for an order sheet. If you don't know what you are looking for, just give them a call.

Colonial Garden Kitchens

Post Office Box 66

Hanover, PA 17333-0066

800/245-3399 (Credit card order only); For information: 800/258-6702

This company offers a wide variety of cooking and baking supplies. They have a tempered glass gugelhupf mold, old-fashioned stoneware mixing bowls, Pyrex double boilers, a tomato seeder, canning supplies, several different brands of pots and pans, cutting boards, and knives. Call for a catalog.

Dean & DeLuca's

560 Broadway

New York, NY 10012

212/431-1691

Dean & DeLuca's carries a large assortment of smoked meats and sausages, game meats and birds, imported and domestic cheeses, oils, vinegars, fruit preserves and syrups, heirloom beans, exotic rices, dried herbs and spices, French yeast for baking, and baking utensils. If you don't see it in the catalog, call and ask.

Delicatessen Meyer

4750 North Lincoln Avenue

Chicago, IL 60625

312/561-3377

Meyer's carries a wide variety of sausages and smoked meats, many imported and domestic cheeses, smoked and pickled fish, ryes and pumpernickels, imported baking supplies, honeys, jams, and coffees,

*as well as chocolates and packaged cookies from all parts of Europe.
Noodles, premade, dried spaetzle, and molds to make dumplings
are available. The company also offers a wide selection of wines,
beers, and liqueurs. Call for a catalog.*

European Sausage House (Szalay Brothers)
4361 North Lincoln Avenue
Chicago, IL 60618
312/472-9645

*If you are a reasonable distance from Chicago, definitely visit this
store if you are looking for outstanding smoked meat products,
from a succulent veal Wiener Würstl to a great smoked ham made
to taste like the hams of half a century ago. The shop carries an
interesting line of European imports, including European cheeses,
mineral waters, honeys, and so forth.*

European Sausage Specialties
12926 Saticoy Street, No. 12
North Hollywood, CA 91605
818/982-2325

*A wide assortment of smoked meats and sausages. Call for an order
form.*

Fácán European Delicatessen
7862 Santa Monica Boulevard
Los Angeles, CA 90046
213/848-8160

*An assortment of smoked meats and sausages, jams, fruit butters,
Hungarian noodles, poppy seed, and paprika.*

Festive Foods
Post Office Box 49172
Colorado Springs, CO 80949-9172
719/594-6768   Fax: 719/522-1672
Contact: Hank (one of the owners)

*This company offers French yeast, Callebaut chocolate for bakers,
nut pastes, flavoring extracts, specialty sugars, dried herbs and
spices in bulk, beans and rices, coffees and teas, dried mushrooms,
oils and vinegars, and dried fruit. Hank, the owner, asked us to say
that "if it isn't in the catalog, please call anyway." He has sources
all over the world, and if it's a food item he'll try like hell to find it!
And probably will!*

Hungarian Trade Commission
130 East Randolph Street
Chicago, IL 60601

312/856-0274   Fax: 312/856-1080
Contact: Assistant to the Commercial Counselor
If you ever have any questions about where to buy Hungarian things in the U.S., call them. They will request information from other Hungarian trade commissions, from New York to California if need be, and will send the information to you ASAP.
K & S European Deli
2229 Huntington Drive
Durate, CA 91010
818/359-0033
An assortment of smoked meats and sausages.
Kerekes
Bakery and Restaurant Equipment, Inc.
7101 13th Avenue
Post Office Box B24
Brooklyn, NY 11228
718/232-7044   Fax: 718/232-4416
Outside NYC: 800/525-5556
A wonderful source for all of your baking and cooking hardware needs. From marzipan molds to fluted pans for all sizes of gugel-hupfs. They also have wooden spoons and rubber spatulas in all sizes. If you have a need for a stainless steel table or sink or parts for your Hobart mixer, you can find it in their catalog. If you don't see it in the catalog, give them a call and they probably have it.
Kuhn's Delicatessen
749 Golf Road
Des Plaines, IL 60016
708/640-0222
Kuhn's offers a wide variety of smoked meats and sausages, imported and domestic cheeses, ryes and pumpernickels, imported cookies, candied fruit peel, nut pastes, baking supplies, honeys, jams and preserves, teas and coffees, spices and dried herbs, imported beers, wines and liqueurs, and mineral waters.
Lahners Imports, Inc.
Specializing in Hungarian Seasoning
8306 Wilshire Boulevard, No. 1549
Beverly Hills, CA 90211
310/659-8723
They carry paprika cream, goulash cream, garlic cream, and red onion cream.

The Market Place Foodstore
393 East Illinois Street
Chicago, IL 60611
312/321-9400
Contact: Peter Stellas
Peter said that they don't have a catalog, but if customers call with requests and the store has it in stock, Market Place will gladly mail the order to them. They carry a wide range of imported food items.
Magyar Marketing
1070 South Schenley Avenue
Youngstown, OH 44509
216/792-7851   Fax: 216/792-7851
Magyar Marketing offers dumpling makers and "Csiga boards" (to make "gander throat" pasta), imported Hungarian noodles, paprika and other spices, several Hungarian salamis and smoked meats, Hungarian cookbooks, and preserves and jams. They also carry an assortment of gift items from Hungary, such as videos, tapes, and books.
Paulina Market
3501 North Lincoln Avenue
Chicago, IL 60657
312/248-6272
Contact: Jerome
The Paulina Market makes all of their sausages by hand and smokes meats and sausages on the premises. Their smoked meats are sent only by next day delivery. Some imported food items which they carry are not listed, so call and ask, and if they have it they'll ship it.
Spiceland
3206 North Major Avenue
Chicago, IL 60634
312/736-1000 (information only); to place an order:
800/352-8671
Fax: 312/736-1217
This small but excellent spice wholesaler and retailer carries a large assortment of the freshest, top quality dried herbs and spices. Not the size of their warehouse but the integrity and expertise of the owners makes them as outstanding as they are.

Williams-Sonoma
Mail Order Department
Post Office Box 7456
San Francisco, CA 94120-7456
800/541-2233

Williams-Sonoma is a good source for hard-to-find baking and cooking equipment and utensils like food mills and cherry pitters, rolling pins that you can fill with ice to keep your dough cold when rolling, and heavy-bottomed pots and pans. They also carry some dried herbs and spices, vinegars and oils, glazed apricots, and fruit syrups. Call to inquire if you don't see it in the catalog.

❧ INDEX ❧

Page numbers in italics refer to entries in the "Notes" section; page numbers in bold refer to entries in the "Bring Vienna to your Table!" section.

cabinet slices, 100; cheese cake, 96; cherries Mannheim, 102; cherry, 82; chocolate cake slices, 103; chocolate cream slices, 77; chocolate roll, 91; chocolate slices with whipped cream, 98; fruit cake, 91; gingerbread à l'Elise (Nürnberg), 104; grape, 101; Gugelhupf, 74, 105, **186**; Hohensalzburg, 91; Linzer torte, **187–189**; mocha cream bars, 95; Napoleon bars, 85; Napoleon cakes, **182**; nut bars with whipped cream, 96; nut roll, 90, **185**; plum pudding, 100; Sacher torte, 98, **198**; sand, 75, 76, 81; Sicilian, 86, **195**; sour cherry bars, 98; sponge cake puffs, 83; sponge cake with meringue, 93; Stephanie slices, 91; stirred sponge, 81; sugar dough for small tarts or strawberry cake, 96; tea cakes, 104; vanilla cream cakes, 99; velvet, 100; white almond, 98; white gingerbread, 104; yeast dough raisin, 75, **175**. *See also* Gâteau; Pastry

Camérani, potage, 57, **159**

Candies: genuine Baden coffee candies, 83

Capon trifle, 61

Capsicum, **126**

Caraway seed liqueur, 103

Carrots with dill in cream sauce, **151**

Caul fat (crépine), *109*

Champignon: garnish, 65; puree, **138**

Chantilly, *112*

Chaudeau, 77, *115*

Cheese: cake, 96; gervais, 84; soufflé, 52

Cherries: brown cherry cake, 94; cake, 82; Mannheim, 102; sour cherry bars, 98; sour cherry ice, 74

Chestnut: bombe, 78; cream gâteau, 100; gâteau, 80; pudding, 75

Chicken: blanquette, *112*; casserole, 53; croustades Colbert, 137; eggs, reine, 56; hash croquettes, 68; hash omelette, 69; hash with egg, 69; mousselines, 145; puree, 137; ragout, Pompadour, 71; risotto, 162–164; rissoles, 68; soup Poligny, 58

Chocolate: bread, 85; cake slices, 103; cold chocolate soufflé, 78; cream slices, 77; crescents, 82; gâteau, 88; pudding, 81, 102; roll, 91; slices with whipped cream, 98

Choux à la crème. *See* Cream puffs

Cinnamon cookies, 80

Clarified sugar, *115*

Clarifying with egg white, *111*

Coffee: cream gâteau, 100; genuine Baden coffee candies, 83; liqueur, 85; praline bombe, 78; pudding, 75, 96

Colbert, Jean Baptiste, *110*

Cookies: cinnamon, 80; English biscuits, 80; gingerbread, 79; gingerbread rounds (Pfeffernüsse), 95; hazelnut stars, 104; little wreaths, 76; Sarah Bernhardt, 82; snowballs, 76; vanilla crescents, 77, **178**; white gingerbread, 104

Cornets, *116*

Coupe Jacques, 73

Crayfish: crépinettes 50; mousse, 49; salad, 82

Cream puffs (choux à la crème), 94

Creams: almond, 82; basic vanilla, **194**; English whip, 81; parfait Fürst Pückler, 90, **183–185**; pistachio, 83, **180**; Russian, 81; vanilla Bavarian, 88

Crépinettes, crayfish, 50

Crescents: almond, 72; chocolate, 82; nut, 96; vanilla, 77, **178**

Croquembouche, 87, *116*

Croquettes, *109*; brain, 71; chicken hash, 68; diplomate, 50; fish, 61; russe, 51

Croustades, *108*, **136**; Cap de

Cougère, 51; Colbert, 51, 137;
Dauphine, 50, 51, 138; with ham
soufflé; 49; plover eggs, Rohan,
51, 138; short dough for, 51;
Strassbourg, 50, 138; Talleyrand,
49
Currant gâteau, 102

Debrecen, 114
Demi-glaze, 108
Duckling à la voisine, 60
Dumplings: Bohemian, 84; bread,
154; cabbage, 54

Eggs: américaine, 55, 174; anchovy, 134; garnish, 64; hors
d'oeuvres, 59; impériale, 56,
173; little plover nests, 50; Mazarin, 56; Meyerbeer, 56; Nelson, 56; opéra, 56; parmesan garnish, 65; plover eggs, Rohan, 51,
138; punch, 103; reine, 56, 173;
Rossini, 55; timbale, Agnes Sorel,
50; timbale, plover eggs, 51
English pie, 82
English whip, 81
Espagnole sauce, 111, 208
Esterházy, 115
Esterházy gâteau, 103

Fish: baveuses, 60; croquettes, 61;
sole américaine, 64; turbot filet
ostendaise, 64
Forcemeat, 108; quenelles, 62, 140
Frankfurters, 140
Fritto misto, 53
Fruit: cake, 91; cherries Mannheim,
102; coupe Jacques, 73; fruit in
cognac, 84; granita of strawberries, 85; ice in wine, 88; peaches,
84; peaches and raspberries, 84;
piquant, 93, 196

Gabelfrühstück, 128, 129
Game: omelette St. Hubert, 55;
pudding, 52, 61; puree, brown,
112
Garnish à la royale, 113
Gâteau: chestnut, 80; chestnut

cream, 100; chocolate, 88; coffee
cream, 100; dark Linzer, 86; Esterházy, 103; with foam topping,
90; genuine Pischinger, 88, 182;
hard currant, 102; hard hazelnut, 99; hard Linzer, 80; Linzer,
97, 187–189; macaroon, 93;
Napoleon, 102; Paris, 97; rum,
99; Russian punch, 97; sand, 86;
sugar dough for fruit gâteau, 96;
Trieste, 99; walnut, 88
Genoa sauce, 65
Gervais cheese, 84
Gingerbread, 79; Elise (Nürnberg),
104; rounds (Pfeffernüsse), 95;
white, 104
Glaze: lemon, 180; punch, 75; rum
icing, 99
Goose: jellied, 55, 168–170; potted ground, 170
Goose liver: croustades Gutenberg,
49; croustades Strasbourg, 138;
eggs impériale, 56; how to cook,
52; omelette Gutenberg, 56;
pâté, 63; patty shells, 53; pudding, 63; ragout, 62; Strasbourg
pâté, 65
Goulash: Andrássy, 68; cowboy's
meat, 66; Debrecen, 66, 165;
gypsy, 67; Holstein, 68; Hungarian, 164; Japanese, 62; kettle, 68;
Paprikash, 164; Stephanie, 68;
supreme, 165; Székely, 68, 165;
Troppau, 67
Granita, 116; strawberries, 85
Grape cake, 101
Gugelhupf, 105, 186; Rothschild,
74, 105; very good, 74
Gutenberg, Johann, 112

Hamburg salad, 62
Hazelnut: bread, 85, 195; gâteau,
99; ice cream, 87; pudding, 90;
stars, 104
Hodge-podge, 52
Hohensalzburg, 117
Holstein, à la, 115
Hors d'oeuvres, egg, 59
Horseradish, apple, 153

THE IOWA SZATHMÁRY CULINARY ARTS SERIES

America Eats
By Nelson Algren

The Cincinnati Cookbook:
Household Guide Embracing Menu, Daily Recipes, Doctors
Prescriptions and Various Suggestions for the Coming Generation
Edited by David E. Schoonover

The Khwan Niamut:
or, Nawab's Domestic Cookery
Edited by David E. Schoonover

P.E.O. Cook Book: Souvenir Edition
Edited by David E. Schoonover

Receipts of Pastry and Cookery:
For the Use of His Scholars
By Edward Kidder

To Set before the King:
Katharina Schratt's Festive Recipes
Edited by Gertrud Graubart Champe